# Aliens and Fakes

Also by Esther Pasztory

Conversations with Quetzalcoatl and Other Stories

Jean-Frederic Waldeck: Artist of Exotic Mexico

Inka Cubism: Reflections on Andean Art

Remove Trouble from Your Heart

Thinking with Things: Toward a New Vision of Art

Daughter of the Pyramids: Colonial Tales

Pre-Columbian Art

Teotihuacan: An Experiment in Living

Aztec Art

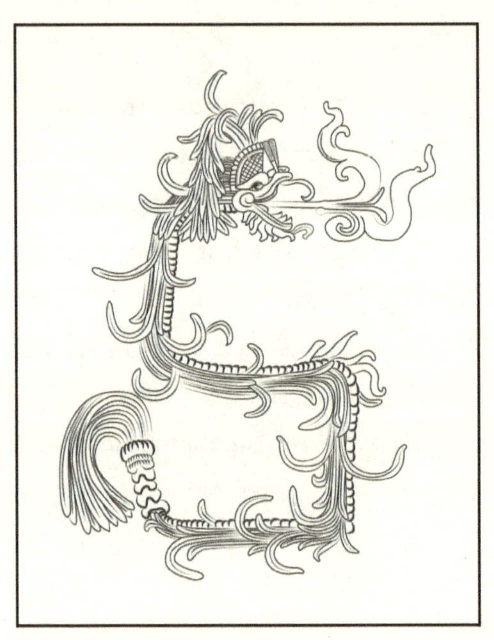

# Aliens and Fakes

## Popular Theories about the Origins of Ancient Americans

Esther Pasztory

Illustrated by Lois Martin

Foreword by David Freedberg

Introduction by William A. Haviland

Polar Bear & Company
Solon, Maine

For Sabina and Alexander

---

My gratitude goes to Lisa and Bernard Selz and to Georgia and Michael de Havenon, who graciously supported the publication of this book.

---



First edition 2015
First printing September 2015

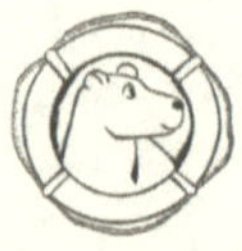

Polar Bear & Company™ is an imprint of
the Solon Center for Research and Publishing
PO Box 311, Solon, Maine 04979 U.S.A.
207.643.2795 www.polarbearandco.org

Library of Congress Control Number: 2015948482
ISBN: 978-1-882190-73-7

Cover design by Emily Cornell du Houx
Illustrations, including Aztec Calendar Stone on cover, by Lois Martin
Manufactured on acid-free paper in more than one country.

# Contents


| | | |
|---|---|---|
| List of Illustrations | | ix |
| Foreword | | xi |
| Introduction | | xiii |
| I | American Indians | 1 |
| II | Princess Watahwaso's Teepee | 4 |
| III | Aliens | 8 |
| IV | The Lost Tribes of Israel | 15 |
| V | Sunken Continents | 22 |
| VI | Racial Migrations | 27 |
| VII | Seagoing Craft | 33 |
| VIII | The Asiatic Tiger | 40 |
| IX | Great Fakes | 47 |
| X | The Question of Indian Identity | 57 |
| XI | What One Needs to Know About Ancient American Art | 64 |
| Mesoamerica | | 67 |
| The Aztec Calendar Stone | | 68 |
| The Olmec Colossal Heads (San Lorenzo 1) | | 70 |
| The Pyramid of the Sun at Teotihuacán | | 72 |
| The Sarcophagus of Pacal at Palenque | | 74 |
| Temples of Tikal | | 76 |
| Chichén Itzá | | 78 |
| The Codex Borgia | | 80 |
| The Andes | | 82 |
| The khipu (Quipu) | | 83 |
| Moche Portrait Heads | | 84 |
| The Paracas Textile | | 86 |
| The Nazca Lines | | 88 |
| The Gate of the Sun, Tiahuanaco | | 89 |
| Sicán Gold Mask | | 90 |
| Machu Picchu | | 92 |
| Epilogue | | 94 |
| Bibliography | | 97 |
| Author | | 103 |

# Illustrations


| | |
|---|---|
| Quetzalcoatl | frontispiece |
| 1. Princess Watahwaso's Teepee | 4 |
| 2. Astronaut in a spaceship? | 8 |
| 3. Quetzalcoatl, the Feathered Serpent | 15 |
| 4. World map showing Atlantis and Mu | 22 |
| 5. Colossal Olmec stone head | 27 |
| 6. Classical period trireme | 33 |
| 7. Chinese junk | 34 |
| 8. Polynesian outrigger canoe | 35 |
| 9. Viking ship | 36 |
| 10. *Kon-Tiki* | 36 |
| 11. The *Ra* | 37 |
| 12. Chou period bronze tiger | 40 |
| 13. Chavin style stone mortar from Peru | 41 |
| 14. Scroll design from a Chinese bronze vessel | 42 |
| 15. Scroll design from El Tajín stone relief in Mexico | 42 |
| 16. Scroll design from a slate mirror back | 43 |
| 17. Stone mask of the Aztec flayed god, Xipe | 47 |
| 18. Greenstone birthgiving goddess | 51 |
| 19. Crystal skull | 54 |
| 20. The Aztec Calendar Stone | 69 |
| 21. Olmec colossal head | 71 |
| 22. Teotihuacan Pyramid of the Sun | 72 |
| 23. Sarcophagus of Pacal at Palenque | 74 |
| 24. Tikal Temple I | 76 |
| 25. Chichén Itzá view of the Castillo | 78 |
| 26. Codex Borgia | 80 |
| 27. The Inca khipu | 83 |
| 28. Moche portrait head vessel | 85 |
| 29. Paracas Textile | 86 |
| 30. Paracas Textile, personage from the fringe detail | 87 |
| 31. Lines in the Nazca Plateau | 88 |
| 32. Tiahuanaco Gate of the Sun | 89 |
| 33. Gold mask, Sicán culture | 91 |
| 34. View of Machu Picchu | 92 |

# Foreword

A wonderful book about the myths and theories, some plausible and some preposterous, that have accumulated over the ages about the origins of the peoples of ancient America. Esther Pasztory treats them all with wisdom and wit. They range from the scientific and pseudo-scientific to the plain outlandish, from migrations from outer space to difficult and sometimes impossible journeys across the earth. Throughout her illuminating account, Pasztory is evenhanded and patient, not only with her teachers who fell for such theories but also with filmmakers like Steven Spielberg and Mel Gibson, who exploited some of the more fantastic theories for their own popular and commercial purposes. Pasztory sees through them all. More than anyone, she realizes that such myths are nothing less than "a vast Rorschach test," as she puts of it, for Westerners' fantasies about the origins of the American Indian.

But there is much more here, too. In this book, readers will also find an accessible account of once completely misjudged (and misdated) Olmec heads and a gripping description of a series of once well-known works of Aztec and Mayan art that have turned out to be fakes (often exposed thanks to her own persistence in the face of curators and professors, who have held out for their authenticity). Such works, she shows, fit all too conveniently into even trained authorities' notions of the cultures from which they were supposed to have emerged.

If all this were not enough, Esther Pasztory, turns her conclusion into the most readable introduction we now have of what everyone needs to know about ancient American art. Nothing could be a more appealing and acute entry into the subject as a whole.

David Freedberg, Pierre Matisse Professor.
Director of the Casa Italiana at Columbia University,
author of *The Power of Images: Studies in the History and Theory of Response*

# Introduction

Ever since Columbus stumbled into the Western Hemisphere, Europeans (and their descendants in the Americas) have been trying to figure out where the inhabitants of these "new" (to Europeans) lands fit into the overall scheme of things. Who were they? how do they relate to other human beings? and what were their capabilities? Could they really have created the great works of art and architecture that even today impress people all over the world, without the help of outsiders?

Over the centuries since Columbus, there has been no end of attempts to answer these questions. Proposals have ranged all the way from Lost Tribes of Israel to refugees from sunken continents, voyagers from (choose one): Phoenicia, Egypt, China, or even Europe itself, to space aliens. Some have even questioned the very humanity of the American Indians. Today or course we have answers to these questions from the world of science. Nevertheless, competing nonscientific theories still enjoy a good deal of popularity, especially those invoking visitors from outer space. We may, perhaps, forgive the thinkers of pre-scientific ages for theories that seem "far out" today; they seemed to make sense to people in the European world at the time. But why, today, do similarly farfetched ideas enjoy the popularity that they do?

This last question is one asked by Esther Pasztory in this book. Dr. Pasztory is a highly respected art historian with an international reputation in the field of pre-Columbian art. She is especially well known for her work at the ancient city of Teotihuacán in Central Mexico. Having spent a long career studying the works of the great civilizations of the Americas, no one is better qualified than she to provide an answer.

As Pasztory points out, all of the theories that purport to explain the presence and accomplishments of the indigenous peoples of the Americas have one thing in common: they tell us much about ourselves and how our biases influence what we see in others. This is certainly true of the most far-out theories, but to a degree it is true of supposedly objective scientific theories as well. Moreover, the creation of fake art objects demonstrates the same point. The ones that have been the most successful are those designed to be as we want to see them, not as indigenous artists would make them. Indeed, Native performers in "wild West" shows and other Indian entertainments, such as Princess Watahwaso (see Chapter 2), have taken advantage of popular stereotypes, giving White audiences what they expected to see and hear, as opposed to what was authentic. For the performers, it was a way of surviving in an alien world. To borrow a phrase from anthropologist Harald Prins, it was "a subversive strategy of creative resistance in the form of theatrics."

I fully concur with Pasztory's analysis. There is, indeed, a thread of racism that runs through these various theories. This is that American Indians are simply not smart enough to accomplish anything worthwhile on their own. If they built great cities with impressive architecture, someone from Europe, Asia, or outer space must have shown them how. Nor could they have produced stunning works of art on their own. In the course of my own career, I have seen many examples of such attitudes. In the state of Maine, for example, Indians had the legal status of "imbeciles" and so were regarded as wards of the state; individuals could not even control their personal assets, requiring permission from an Indian agent to do anything with them. So you have incidents like one experienced by the nephew of Princess Watahwaso. A genuine hero of World War II, after the war was over, he went with his family into Old Town, Maine, to vote in a local ejection. At the head of the line, wearing his dress uniform studded with medals for bravery under fire and capture by the enemy, he was told, "Idiots don't have the right to vote in this state."

Even supposedly objective scientists have been blinded by their cultural biases. Nothing illustrates this better than the study of the ancient Maya civilization of southern Mexico and northern Central America. When I went to work at Tikal (see Chapter 11), now a UNESCO World Heritage Site, scholars were convinced that this and other Maya ruins, with impressive temples and other monuments, were "empty" ceremonial centers. Having no resident population, they were visited periodically by simple peasants, living scattered in the forests, to build, maintain, and carry out ceremonies in the buildings. What this view reflected were three biases on the part of the scholars, as well as a bit of wishful thinking.

To take the biases first: For one, the Maya ruins were in a heavily forested area, and to Europeans forests are not friendly places. Wild animals live in them, and in European folklore, they are places where the forces of evil hang out and bad things happen (think "Little Red Riding

Hood" or "Hansel and Gretel"). They are places of darkness, and the English language is rich in metaphors about "beating back the forest" or "letting the sunlight in." Given such negative feelings, how could anyone create a complex civilization in such an inhospitable setting? To make matters worse, these weren't just any forests, they were tropical forests. To northern people, the tropics were seen as hostile climates, where people were debilitated by the heat and humidity. Furthermore, they are environments in which malaria and other tropical diseases ran rampant! Strike two against the Maya!

The third bias stemmed from the historic Maya practice of slash-and-burn farming, a "low tech" operation requiring that farmers shift their fields every few years over extensive areas as fertility was exhausted. The assumption was that their ancient forbears relied on the same system. Such a system was regarded as "primitive" (today we know better) and incapable of supporting the large, complex populations required for civilization. Strike three against the Maya!

As for the wishful thinking, the twentieth century with all its turmoil and conflicts inspired a longing for some kind of idyllic, peaceful society. In the ancient Maya, many thought they had found just that. The idea of peaceful peasants scattered about in their forest, devoting themselves to the contemplation of time and observations of the heavens, as their inscriptions seemed to suggest, fit neatly with the other biases.

Unlike pop theories, of course, long-standing hypotheses are constantly reexamined by scientists in the light of new evidence. Although it may take a while, science is self-correcting, and theories shown to be incorrect are ultimately discarded. At Tikal, work by myself and others in the 1960s demonstrated that the place was a large and diverse city. Others have gone on to show that the Maya employed varied and sophisticated systems of agriculture. And far from being peaceful philosophers of time, we now know that the Maya were as bloody minded as other civilizations, as Maya kings were constantly launching attacks against rivals in other cities.

To return to the pop theories, part of the problem, as Pasztory sees it, is a widespread ignorance in the Americas today about the continent's past. This is all the more surprising, given all that Indians have contributed to the world (think corn, beans, squash, potatoes, tomatoes, and avocados, to name just a few). In fact, the very survival of the early American colonies would not have been possible without knowledge gained from the Native people. In view of this ignorance, Pasztory lays out a list of what everyone should know about ancient American art. I applaud her efforts and suggest that every reader of this book take a quiz, to see how many of these things she or he knows about.

To be fair, widespread ignorance about this hemisphere's past is at least in part the fault of scholars. Much of their writing is aimed not at a general audience but at each other, in ways that make what they have to say inaccessible to outsiders. In their defense, they do so because in the academic world the rewards are distributed to those who write for specialist journals and presses, not to those who write for the general public. I am happy to say that Esther Pasztory is an exception to this rule. She has done her fair share of "professional" writing, but as this book demonstrates, she can write for a wider audience as well.

William A. Haviland
Professor Emeritus of Anthropology
University of Vermont

# I

# AMERICAN INDIANS

When Columbus discovered the Americas, he thought he was in Asia, near India or China, and named the people he met "Indians," a confusion that has not been untangled even in our times. We therefore refer to the original inhabitants of the New World as "American Indians" or, being politically correct, "Native Americans." Most American Indians refer to themselves usually as "Indians" or "American Indians," since they have no other collective term for themselves as a people. They refer to themselves either by specific tribal names or by location. It is people from the outside, namely Westerners, who see them as a general category of beings that need a name.

The biological and racial affiliation of the American Indian has been similarly confused. Europeans were used to Africans, Middle Easterners and Asians ("Orientals"), but American Indians did not fit into either of those categories. They were a little similar both to Europeans and to Asians, but eventually their skin color, a reddish brown, gave them the epithet of being "red men." However, there is enough ambiguity in the physiognomy of American Indians to have served all kinds of theories about European, Chinese, African, or Polynesian "origins" for them. The essential point is that Native Americans have not been easily classified as a race, and, technically, may not be a distinct and homogeneous race. Because of this apparent racial ambiguity, from the beginning of the conquests in the sixteenth century it was possible for Europeans to think that they were people like them and that the repository of knowledge in the Bible could refer to them. From the beginning it was possible to imagine that they were not autochthonous but that they came from somewhere else. The information culled from the Bible was that they were most likely the Ten Lost Tribes of Israel and were therefore immigrants of Jewish origins. Since that time to the present, one of the major pastimes of amateurs and scholars has been to surmise who were the American Indians and where they might have come from.

The orthodox twentieth-century scholarly position has been that they were Asians who came across the Bering Straits about thirteen thousand years ago in one major migration and divided to local groups in the Americas. Because this time was the Ice Age, there was a land bridge between northern Asia and America, and people went across on foot. The existence of an ice-free corridor allowed them to move into the lower reaches of the Americas. The fluted projectile points of these migrant people were named Clovis, and some Clovis points were associated with the kill of mammoths and other Paleolithic animals. Accordingly, it is believed that the original migrants into the Americas were big-game hunters. This analysis has not stopped other theories from flourishing, including the one that the Indians are extraterrestrials.

A major new source of information has come from the DNA testing of modern Indians populations and ancient bone remains. More than seven thousand people have been tested showing that American Indians fall into four mitochondrial DNA groups, labeled ABCD, which are close to Siberian Asian types, as the migration theory suggests. However, the DNA tests demonstrated a fifth category, labeled "X," which is not Asian. This category has parallels with Polynesian types, and, to a very small extent, with European ones. Most interestingly, recent excavations in both North and South America unearthed skeletons and tools from before the Clovis level. The skulls found there are longer and narrower than the broad Clovis-era skulls and more comparable to those of Europeans, Polynesians, and the Ainu of Japan.

Based on the DNA findings and recent archaeology, scientists now suggest that before the Clovis migration from Siberia, there might have been some migrants to the Americas from throughout the circum-Pacific regions. As there was no land bridge at that time, people must have come by boat. The use of relatively sophisticated boats goes back twenty to forty thousand years ago in Southeast Asia. As the popular theorists were never satisfied by a single, unified migration but looked for a variety of parallels, these new findings offer many possibilities of interpretations.

Why should the origin of the American Indian be such a source of fascination for over four hundred years? I propose that many theorists saw themselves or their idea of civilization in the American Indian and wanted to be a part of it. Like the gold rushes in the New World, some Europeans also wanted to possess the American Indian for their particular religious or intellectual purposes. Assigning the American Indian to a particular culture in the Old World or even to extraterrestrials was to integrate them into the Western world (after all, the mere idea of extraterrestrials is Western). By integrating the Indian into the West, the conquest of the Americas could be legitimized on ideological as well as biological grounds. This account of some of the theories regarding the origins of the American Indian is not so much to ridicule the misguidedness of these undertakings, but is more an examination of what motivated people in their search and what they hoped to accomplish. As with all scholars, too, popular theorists were bound by the limits of the ideas of their times. There is evidence that despite greater scientific knowledge, in the twenty-first century imaginative reconstructions of the origins of humankind have not come to an end.

# II

# PRINCESS WATAHWASO'S TEEPEE

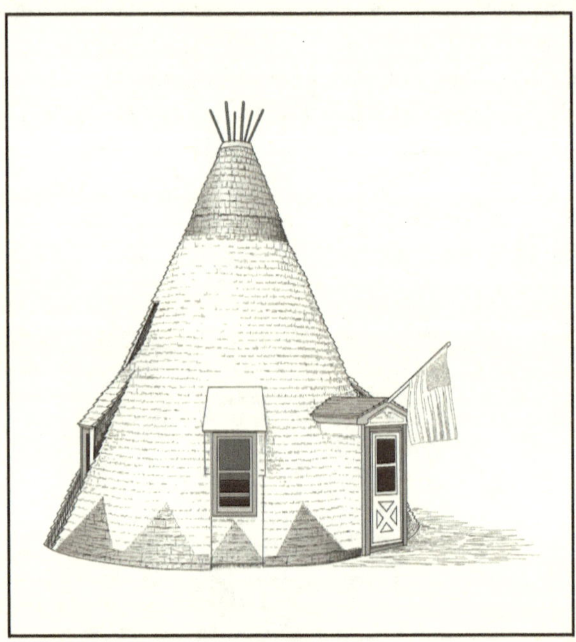

Fig. 1. Princess Watahwaso's Teepee on the Penobscot Indian Reservation.

Were the Native Americans aliens from outer space? the Lost Tribes of Israel? survivors of Atlantis? or Chinese explorers? Were they racially White, Asian, or Black? Why do many people believe that Native Americans came from some exotic place and have a hidden identity? In the pages that follow, I will mention many of the popular theories about the origins of Native American culture, pointing out their reasonable and unreasonable aspects and focusing on their contexts. The theories themselves are a testament to the deep popular fascination of people in the West with the New World and its inhabitants, which goes much beyond scientific inquiry. By way of conclusion, I will describe some of the major monuments of ancient American art that everyone needs to know.

This book sketches some of the myths about Native Americans and their spectacular ruins, as generations of Europeans and Americans tried to make sense of them. While it is focused on Mesoamerica and the Andes with their fantastic monuments, the Indian question cannot be discussed apart from other Indians, such as the well-known North American tribes. To many writers past and present, Indians are Indians, wherever they are, and we easily equate them with one another. Sometimes I will have to do the same. Similarly, though the ruins and monuments belong to the past, or at least were prior to 1500 AD, it is impossible to discuss them entirely without reference to contemporary Indians. Contemporary Indians have been a part of modern culture for centuries and maintain their own histories and identities. The subject of the origins of "Indians" is therefore difficult to limit either in space or time, and I have limited it arbitrarily in focusing on the main issues of the popular theories.

The popular theorists about Indian identity either had no access to "official" or "scientific" histories about them, were not satisfied by such official histories, or there were no official histories available, a situation that has made their imaginations soar above and beyond the probable or possible. Such myths include the identity of the Indians as the Lost Tribes of Israel or of aliens from outer space. Less remote but just as problematic are theories about Atlantis and diffusion from China. Most official scholars disregard all these ideas as absurdities not worth mentioning and don't mention them. Occasionally there is an interesting study, such as Wauchope's *Lost Tribes and Sunken Continents*, which presents but also ridicules mercilessly the proponents of such ideas. I am not interested in easy ridicule, but in explanation. Why have people come up with such notions since the sixteenth century and do so until today? Do the theories have any merit, even if a non-scholarly one? Can we recognize that these theories are as much a part of the field as the scientific explanations?

A more sympathetic reading of the material reveals two interrelated strands of ideas. The first is that given the state of knowledge and ideas at the time, many of these theories were not as unreasonable as hindsight makes them out. Or, between two unreasonable possibilities often the more "reasonable" was selected, given current sources and methods, which is why some of these myths have had such longevity. A second reason for the myths is the lack of knowledge within the general population about Indians and their ruins. A lack of accurate information was certainly true in the early centuries, after the sixteenth-century conquest, but despite much recent research, popular lack of information remains true today. Yet ordinary people are interested in and fascinated by Indians and their monuments. Many more people are interested in Indians, in fact, than those who wish and can do the research about them. What we know about Greece and Rome we learned in school. But in school we did not learn about the Inca and Maya, because Native civilizations generally are not taught in the US. People pick up their information from Western movies, shamanic cults, and Indian casinos. As the knowledge about Native Americans is more or less a vacuum, it is easy to fill it with spaceships and aliens. The idea of aliens is particularly logical, in a way, in that it recognizes the high intellectual level of ancient cultures, while identifying their makers as mysterious outsiders.

Most scholars complain that all these elaborate ideas take creativity away from the Indian to assorted Jewish, Chinese and alien outsiders. They make the Indian seem slow-witted and stupid. I think that these speculations indicate that though there is a fascination with Indians, so little is known about them that they are compared to something very special and unfamiliar. Indian identity is a mystery in the popular imagination. Yet people want to know about Indians but don't know where to start. There is certainly no one to speak for the ancient ruins, except for the official scholars, whose ideas are often inaccessible and unfulfilling in bits and pieces.

Scholars often point out that the makers of the great monuments are the ancestors of the mostly peasant, modern-day surviving Indians, who are in the same breath not given credit for the works of their ancestors. In fact, relating these modern groups to the ancient monuments is a daunting task, even for the specialists. Matching up language groups, ethnic customs, physical appearance, with monuments is full of pitfalls. When it is done on the popular level, as by Mel Gibson in *Apocalypto*, the awkwardness and the anachronisms are simplistic and neither beautiful nor profound. He can be congratulated for trying. Most filmmakers don't even try.

Some contemporary Indians send up smoke signals of communication. For example one family on Indian Island, on the Penobscot Reservation in Maine, has put up a large teepee commemorating their history: Princess Watahwaso's Teepee. Princess Watahwaso was the romantic stage name of Lucy Nicolar Poolaw, who performed in Indian shows at the turn of the century as "the" Indian maiden. She came from an educated family. Her father, Joseph Nicolar, was a member of the Maine Legislature and published a book, *The Life and Traditions of the Red Man*, in 1893, in which he explored what it is to be an Indian, by an Indian. Lucy's sister Florence was also politically active and was a traditional basketmaker. She and other basketmakers demonstrated their weaving craft in the teepee. The family claimed to be both modern in the modern world and to be Indian in the traditional sense. They seek and sought to communicate their Indianness to the Anglo communities around them. Information on the Penobscots, their history and music, are now on sale in the museum, kept up by a member of the family. The message of Princess Watahwaso's Teepee is that Indians are not just nameless collective tribes but historic individuals and that Indianness is not given with their DNA but something they create out of the circumstances of their lives. One leaves the teepee-museum having a more complex idea of the contradictions and compromises Indians make in today's world and probably did in ancient times as well. Lucy Poolaw appealed to the romantic imagination of Westerners in the identity of Princess Watahwaso, but she would never have appeared on stage as a Jewess, Chinese, or extraterrestrial. These are not Native American myths. While it is exceptionally valuable to have Indians communicate their ideas about themselves, these are modern myths created from the political realities of the present. The present can never be completely kept out of one's view of the past, but the past can be looked at from a less personal view as a forensic field of analysis.

While a visit to Princess Watahwaso's museum would be a learning experience for anyone, it does not take the place of instruction in school about the accomplishments of Indian antiquity. The Indian past would be best interpreted for most people in formal education, giving it the dignity reserved for other cultures introduced that way. Instruction in the differences of Aztec, Maya, and Inca cultures in comparison with Egypt, Mesopotamia, and Asia would put ancient America in a global context as one of the great early civilizations of the world. There would still remain questions about aliens and so forth, because we don't know for sure the cultural interrelationships on earth to say nothing of outer space.

The identities projected on Native Americans by Westerners say more about us than about them and are therefore of great interest to us. They indicate the extent to which—five centuries after the colonization of the Americas—we still have difficulty placing Native Americans in our realistic world schema and resort to fantasy. Each fantasy reveals different aspects of ourselves, as it also questions the limits of scholarly enterprise.

# III

# ALIENS

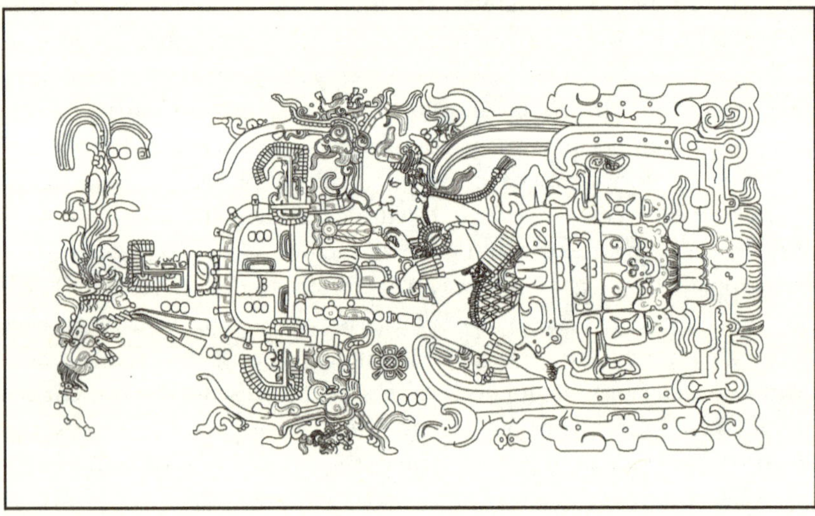

Fig. 2. Astronaut in a spaceship? Drawing of the sarcophagus lid from Palenque, Mexico, turned sideways without some of the border, to show the "astronaut," the Maya king Pacal entering the underworld.

Aliens have always been with us. Ghosts, for example, are as old probably as humanity. Ghosts come back mysteriously from the Planet of Death. They are vague in form, sometimes harmless, sometimes evilly intentioned towards the living. Ghosts are one prototype for extraterrestrials. Aliens are also like incomprehensible foreigners in our midst, who we also call "aliens." They are like us in form but strange in thought and behavior.

UFOs and aliens were first sighted in large numbers after World War II, mostly in the USA. It is assumed that this has to do with the importance of aircraft in the war and subsequently in civil life and the anxious scanning of the skies by the population. Besides all the sudden air traffic in the twentieth century, the bombs exploded over Hiroshima and Nagasaki impressed people with their lethal force and their potential visibility outside the earth. To some they were seen as possible signals to outer space that very intelligent species exist on earth, which might have explained all the sightings of alien space ships. In some science fiction, aliens indeed discover the existence of earth from the atomic blasts. It is popularly assumed that alien civilizations must have had the greatest then-known human power, which is atomic power.

Of the thousands of UFO sightings, a large proportion are misunderstood military maneuvers, stellar phenomena, and a great many have been hoaxes. Some are nevertheless inexplicable phenomena. According to witnesses, most consist of bright lights and abnormally fast movement. There is less of an agreement on the beings inside the spaceships, although some claim to have been abducted by them. Hollywood B movies, especially of the 1950s, gave shape to the aliens, often in semi-human form, for the story to match up with a human protagonist. Also, as Von Däniken argued, the aliens would have to be in roughly human shape, with necessarily two legs to carry themselves around, two arms to carry things in them, and they would have to carry their brains on top like humans in order to see and think. By necessity, in order to get here, aliens would have superhuman technology—with which, in the movies, they threaten the earth. But in the end, humans get the better of them and save the world. Often some curious and enterprising person goes with the aliens, back to their planet, somewhere in outer space.

Ghosts are personal and familial, but aliens are likely to be for or against all humanity, and all humanity is revved up to take care of the incursion. In fact, the only model for an alien invasion on earth is the Spanish Conquistadors, who encountered the thriving empires of the Aztec and Inca in the Americas, in the sixteenth century. The Spanish came to conquer, and in short order they did, with their high technology, territorial imperative, and cunning. This is not an encouraging scenario for contact with those supposedly advanced beings in outer space.

We don't know for certain whether UFOs or aliens exist in reality, but they exist in our mythology. Whether they are mass hallucinations due to the traumas of war and fear of the immensity of the cosmos, as Carl Jung thought in the 1950s, or to scientific preoccupations with space, since Sputnik, Yuri Gagarin's pioneering trip, the subsequent walk on the moon, the space station, and the probes on Mars, is unclear, but we have been preoccupied by space.

Of all the sightings, given that many have been explained away as military secrets, atmospheric phenomena, and hoaxes, some remain genuine puzzles. Everyone agrees that spaceships are supposed to be mostly round, have dazzling lights, and can move at unbelievable speeds. Space gear and travel in our culture have become familiar and even domesticated, and all that detail can be added to the concept of aliens. As a result, the aliens of the imagination have become friendlier, like our astronauts—curious travelers in outer space. In 1977 and 1982, Steven Spielberg made two successful movies about aliens. In *Close Encounters of the Third Kind*, people are irresistibly drawn to the landing of a spaceship, defined by its dramatic lights, and are especially hopeful of seeing the creatures from afar. These remain remote silhouettes. No actual danger to humanity is suggested. Next, *E.T. the Extra-Terrestrial* is even more friendly, where an alien left behind accidentally by a spaceship is befriended by children. The benignity of the visitor is underlined by the fact that the alien has the ability to heal wounds. He is a healer and not an aggressor.

Now that the news and entertainment media have the population used to aliens visiting us from time to time, it appears to many that aliens have been here numerous times before and left their mark on the greatest and most inexplicable monuments of the past, like Stonehenge and the pyramids of Egypt and Mexico. These monuments have previously been attributed to earlier aliens, such as the Lost Tribes of Israel or the survivors of Atlantis, but now become the achievements of helmeted travelers from outer space. By the twenty-first century, aliens are as much a part of popular mythology as Santa Claus and his reindeer. All a moviemaker has to show is a circular craft, and we know it is extraterrestrial.

It was not much of a surprise when the South American Indian "aliens" of *Indiana Jones and the Kingdom of the Crystal Skulls*, the 2008 movie, got off their Maya-style temple pyramid and got into a classically round spaceship and left for parts unknown, towards the end of the story. The creatures' Indian identity had been established by their South American location and by their headquarters, which looked like the Temple of Warriors at Chichén Itzá, with a circular floor that looked like the Aztec Calendar Stone and many other references to famous works of pre-Columbian art, most of which are in Mexico. The South American adventure included the find of many mummies in burial caves, whose ghoulish skulls were to scare the moviegoer. These skulls turned out to be similar to the crystal skull that was sought after and that turned out to be the head of one of the aliens. A parallel was implied between the ancient skulls in the tombs and the more fantastic crystal skulls, between the ghosts from the past and the extraterrestrials of the present. The screenwriters of *Indiana Jones and the Kingdom of the Crystal Skulls* did not venture into new interpretations of the alien myth; they gave form to the already existing popular conceptions. These aliens, too, caused no trouble to humanity in conveniently exiting the earth.

The person who gave form to the alien theory as we know it today is Erich von Däniken, a Swiss hotel manager who published *Chariots of the Gods* in 1967, followed by *Gods from Outer Space*, 1968, *The Gold of the Gods*, 1973, and other books. The German title of *Chariots of the Gods* was *Erinnerungen an die Zukunft* or "Memories of the Future." This book was translated into more than thirty languages, was a bestseller, and made its author a VIP wherever he went.

The gist of von Däniken's theory is that advanced aliens created human civilization on earth and maybe even man himself, bypassing or adapting evolution. They left great works on earth, such as pyramids and occasionally images of themselves. For example, what is interpreted as a Tree of Life and the Maya ruler Pacal on the sarcophagus lid at Palenque by scholars reveals, when turned sideways by von Däniken, an extraterrestrial astronaut peering into a telescope-like instrument. According to his theory, the extraterrestrials came to earth because of a great war in space that they had lost, and they had to flee their enemies and hide somewhere. Because of their superior knowledge and strange gear, people thought that they were gods and worshipped them. In antiquity, the extraterrestrial spaceships were interpreted to be the "chariots" of the gods. The many similarities between people's gods and myths in different cultures are attributed to the fact that they are all based on the arrival of the same aliens.

Much as von Däniken derides scientists as fools and debunks their books, his books are all about science. He quotes Einstein approvingly as an authority and retells the Big Bang theory of the origin of the universe. Some of his theories are not far from ideas held by well-respected scientists. The scientific theory that life came as a spore from outer space had been around since the 1900s, as presented by the Nobel laureate Svante Arrhenius, and a more recent Nobel prize winner, Sir Francis Crick, developed it seriously in the early 1970s. Known as Directed Panspermia, Crick's theory requires a spaceship to bring the spores to earth. Francis Crick received his Nobel with Watson and Wilkens in 1962 for the very mainstream study of the double helix structure of DNA. Other scientists have made various attempts actually to contact aliens. Carl Sagan and Paul Drake created a golden plaque to be attached to Pioneer

10, to communicate with aliens, launched in 1972. On it were "basic" mathematical and astronomical formulae, as well as outline images of a naked man and woman. Perhaps luckily so far, no one has responded to the directions to earth on the plaque. There is plenty of evidence that in the 1960s and 70s there was a lot of interest in extraterrestrial matters in the scientific community, and von Däniken did not seem totally out of step. In fact, he may have encouraged serious scientific probes.

One of von Däniken's most lasting theories was about the Nazca lines—known as geoglyphs to scholars—in southern Peru. On a dry plateau between the Ingenio and Palpa rivers, lines were created by removing the top layer of darker, oxidized stones and revealing the lighter surface underneath. These lines and shapes are mostly geometric, but there are a few animal and plant figures among them. Some of the trapezoids are huge and may be as much as a kilometer long. The mysterious feature of these lines is that they can be mainly seen from the air and only to a limited extent from the ground. They were discovered by Peruvian aviators in the 1920s, and their fame spread outside Peru in the 1940s. The finds of a few pieces of Nazca-style pottery among the lines dated them to the Nazca period, about 500 AD. But there are no habitations or other monuments on the plateau. Initially the lines were presumed to be astronomically oriented, but extensive research disproved that theory. Von Däniken saw the lines of Nazca as a giant airport with the lines and trapezoids as the landing fields for the aliens. He suggested that people made them to attract the aliens. This idea, by now also not new, is casually present in the beginning of *Indiana Jones and the Kingdom of the Crystal Skulls*, where the lines are presented on the way of the protagonists to South America. They signify South America. We know right away that the movie is about popular ideas.

The scholarly community is quite baffled by the lines—currently they are thought to be ritual pathways, cared for by lineages, or near sources of aquifers important in a desert area—but no explanation seems completely right. The most that can be said is that ancient Andean representation often seemed to be what we call "conceptual" and to have dealt more with ideas than visibility and that visibility was not necessarily an important feature. The long lines and figures could have been laid out with ropes and standard measurements.

While von Däniken's idea of the "landing fields" is ridiculous, in a strange way it is the most apt description of the lines and brings them into our world and experience. He has captured some of their mystery and encouraged many to see and write about them. The lines of Nazca may now be as famous as the pyramids of Egypt and are one of the current Seven Wonders of the World.

Von Däniken was impressed by old works that seem to demonstrate that people could see what they could not see. He was fascinated by the early eighteenth-century Piri Reis maps that showed the world in a way that could not have been seen at that time, given that technology—much like the Nazca lines. He argued that the past needed to be seen from the point of view of modern technology. He urges space exploration not just in order to colonize the universe but also for the technological fallout from space research for all aspects of modern life. He does believe in the colonization of the universe and intermarriage with its peoples, if at all possible.

More conventionally, von Däniken was impressed by the huge stones erected in the past—the Easter Island and Olmec heads, the sculptures of Tiahuanaco, and the walls of the Inca. He could not imagine that these stones could have been moved and worked without modern tools, by people he tended to describe as poor savages in loincloths. But these monuments were secondary to his arguments about images that could not even have been seen, like the Nazca lines and the Piri Reis map.

Besides the atmosphere of interest in extraterrestrials in the 1960s and 70s, von Däniken was successful because his books were written in an easy yet "scholarly" style. As well as retelling verifiable scientific facts and experiments, he presented his theories with careful descriptions keyed to illustrations. If you looked up the picture you could see the astronaut's helmet on the figure he pointed out. Granted that the helmet could have other interpretations, his interpretation was visible.

Von Däniken roamed the world to find modern rituals in which figures that were dressed in masks looked like astronauts, and he combed mythologies that included stories of gods (aliens) coming from the sky. I imagine that for many readers these thumbnail sketches of ancient and modern exotic cultures were the closest they had come to reading about most of these cultures. Von Däniken introduced people to reading about other cultures, chiefly those of ancient America. No such book or TV program was available that would have done the same. Not taught in school, and in the absence of more available, orthodox literature, von Däniken's theories proved plausible and desirable for readers worldwide.

The most unpleasant aspects of von Däniken's books are his frequent diatribes against scientists, by whom he means mainly anthropologists, for being unwilling to see his version of the truth. He presents himself as an outsider not appreciated by the scholarly mafia. Since the readers of his books are similarly outsiders, they are likely to sympathize with their author. Moreover, where are the easily comprehensible books written by scholars? Scholars have a tendency to have an explanation for everything, while von Däniken points out their essential mystery and otherness. Actually, von Däniken has written himself into the history of ancient American studies, even if infamously as an important popularizer.

Popular theories about the origins of Indians are sometimes related to religious cults and organizations. Von Däniken's ideas have been incorporated into the sect, Falun Gong, in China, for example. According to its leader, Li Honzhi, Falun Gong is a completely new understanding of human beings in society. Consisting of physical exercises, meditation, and a new historical view of the universe, the sect has seemed politically threatening to the Chinese Communist leadership and is persecuted. Practitioners of Falun Gong believe that there have been many, over eighty, human civilizations, each one of which almost died out to be recreated by a few survivors. As proof of the existence of the early civilizations, they refer to sections of von Däniken's books, such as the relief of a man peering into a telescope from Palenque. Falun Gong adherents believe that this era is coming to an apocalyptic end very soon and will be replaced by another world. While they don't believe in the extraterrestrial theory as such, by separating history into discreet worlds, they are denying the continuity of human cultures and allowing for strange manifestations in the remote past.

By a small leap of thought, the theory of aliens actually reveals an anxiety about the existence of God. For example, Von Däniken agonizes whether God put all these universes with sentient beings into motion or whether they developed automatically by Darwinian evolution. His theory of extraterrestrials does not answer the question of God's existence. Who created them? It shows, however, the close relationship between the question of aliens, even if cast as earlier humanity as in Falun Gong, and religion.

# IV

# THE LOST TRIBES OF ISRAEL

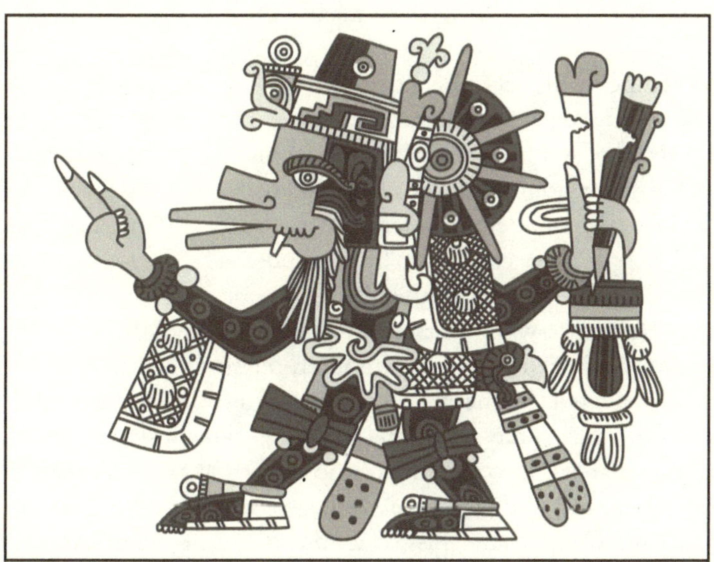

Fig. 3. Quetzalcoatl, the Feathered Serpent from the Codex Borgia, Mexican manuscript. He is shown here as the wind god Ehecatl with a buccal mask. The beard suggested to the Spanish that he might have been a European.

Aliens in the twentieth century are what the Lost Tribes of Israel were for the earlier three or more centuries in explaining the original novelty of ancient American civilization. The racial and ethnic identity of Native Americans was in question from the moment Columbus thought that they were "Indians" from the "East Indies" in 1492, since he did not recognize that America was a different continent from Asia. According to current anthropological theory, humans developed in Africa and migrated from there to Europe and Asia. In the sixteenth century, in the age of conquest and colonization, Europeans had a hard time classifying the American natives racially; they were to them not distinct races, like Whites, Blacks, or Asians, but something in between, and they imagined that Indians had to have come from somewhere in the Old World. Unfortunately, the Bible, which was supposed to tell the story of all humankind and all races did not specifically refer to Native Americans. There was only one story in the Old Testament that referred to a people who had disappeared or who had gone away never to be heard from again, that could have been the Native Americans, and that was the Ten Lost Tribes of Israel. But as all knowledge was supposed to be in the Bible, by a process of elimination those tribes must have been the ones.

Sometime in the eighth century BC, the king of Assyria was said to have captured the ten Lost Tribes of Israel. According to legend, the king encircled them by a river full of rapids, so that they could not cross it to go back to their homeland, and they eventually made their way to other lands. Since then, modern travelers in Asia, Africa and the Americas have "found" peoples they claimed to be descendants of the Lost Tribes. This was especially the case about the Native Americans.

In 1521, Mexico was the first major American kingdom conquered and the place where many theories and interpretations about the American Indians originated. In the sixteenth century in Mexico, the Lost Tribe identification was common among religious scholars such as Bartolomé de las Casas and Diego Durán. We do not know who was the first to start the idea, and it may go back to Cortés and his men. The idea was especially important to the missionary protectors of the Indians, because the major controversy of the day was whether Indians had souls or not. If they had no souls, they could be enslaved and worked to death in the mines, and this was the position of many early settlers. If they had souls, they were fully human, deserved better treatment, and they could be converted to Christianity. A conference in Valladolid, where Bartolomé de las Casas was present, decided that the Indians had souls, which had a lot to do with the idea that they were the descendents of Jews, a people known from the Bible. While the Jews were non-Christians, they had lived among Christians for centuries and were more or less accepted by them as fellow humans. Moreover, Jews were considered to have strange habits not unlike the Indians. Thus the Indians were seen as human and could be converted to Christianity. The label of Lost Tribes was initially a positive one from the point of view of Natives, because it brought them into the orbit of the Bible. Clearly the Indians of Central and South America had impressive monuments and a high civilization in keeping with a supposed Near Eastern identity and deserved a biblical origin.

The idea of "lost" tribes suggests that they were people "lost" to us and thus lost to their real selves. The discovery of the New World brought to light a "lost" continent, lost only to us since "we" claimed it. By the discovery of the continent and its people by "us," they have been restored to us. The theory needed little proof other than the story in the Bible and the claim of kinship with the Indian. Later in the nineteenth century, when the images of Palenque were published, anyone could see for themselves the big Jewish noses on the Maya sculptured figures.

The theory of the Lost Tribes of Israel was found alongside theories of the Egyptians, Phoenicians, Canaanites, Greeks and other ancient peoples as the makers of the Native monuments. Perhaps it was thought that if the Jews could get there, so could others. The theory of the Lost Tribes was not inconsistent with other ancient visitors, but it remained the most popular. It was popular through much of the nineteenth century, and many books were written on one or another aspect of these supposed migrations.

Christian elements had also been seen in the Native cultures since the sixteenth century, giving rise to the idea that Christ or the Apostle St. Thomas in particular had traveled through ancient America, spreading Christianity prior to the conquest by Cortés. Such similarities included the naming ceremony of newborn Aztec children with water, which was seen as similar to Christian baptism. The idea of the spread of Christian beliefs and practices before Columbus is not so strange if we consider that the Indians were Jews, and like the Jews of the Near East, they were converted by Jesus. Jesus or one of his apostles must have converted some of the "Jews" of the New World.

The idea of an earlier Christianizing movement coalesced especially around the figures of two Native gods, Quetzalcoatl of the Aztecs and Viracocha of the Inca, who were supposed to be blonde, light skinned, bearded, and benign. Of the two, the story of Quetzalcoatl was more elaborated.

Quetzalcoatl—or Feathered Serpent—was, according to sixteenth-century colonial myth, the ruler of the city of Tula prior to Aztec times, and he was supposed to have been a monk-like figure, mortifying his own flesh, but not believing in human sacrifice. However, in a moment of weakness, this upright person had sex with the goddess Xochiquetzal and thus committed a sin. Related or unrelated to this sin, he was attacked by a rival faction in the city of Tula, led by the god of darkness, Tezcatlipoca—Smoking Mirror—who drove him from the city and ended his earthly rule. According to some sources, Quetzalcoatl and his followers went to the Gulf Coast, where he built a bonfire, immolated himself, and became the planet Venus. According to other sources, he sailed off on a raft of serpents, vowing that that he'd be back.

Quetzalcoatl's birth date in the Aztec calendar is 1 Reed and the year when Cortés appeared on the scene in 1519 was a 1 Reed year. Analyzing their calendar and histories, some Aztecs may have believed that Cortés was the returning Quetzalcoatl or some other god. They sent him various deity costumes on the ship to see which one he would pick out, therefore who he was, and they hoped he would be satisfied with the gifts and go away. Cortés of course was mainly interested in the gold on the costumes. He was crafty enough to recognize that he was being taken for a god and encouraged the rumor as long as he could. Montezuma himself vacillated between thinking that this was Quetzalcoatl returning to take his empire back—bad enough in itself—and thinking that the Spanish were strange human invaders to be stopped militarily. Neither strategy was applied consistently and neither worked against the superiority of Spanish arms and determination. In either case, Quetzalcoatl played a major ideological role in the conquest—as a myth both the Aztecs and the Spanish could believe in to explain the unbelievable fact of the conquest, as Jacques Lafaye showed.

There is no clear evidence that there was a major religious cult of Quetzalcoatl among the Aztecs prior to the conquest, based on their monuments, nor is there evidence for his importance in the monuments of the city of Tula. There is a connection with the feathered serpent, which is a symbol of fertility and transformation and is commonly represented, but we de not know if the feathered serpent was definitely a symbol of the mythic Quetzalcoatl. According to colonial texts, Quetzalcoatl was a creator god who created mankind and gave them maize, but this is not represented on most pre-Hispanic monuments. It has been suggested that Quetzalcoatl was the patron of a royal investiture ritual centered on the city of Cholula in pre-Aztec and perhaps later times. None of the evidence suggests that the ancient Quetzalcoatl was blond, white skinned, and abhorred human sacrifices. The imagery of the site of Tula and of other sites supposedly related to Quetzalcoatl deal mainly with war and sacrifice.

Much of the Quetzalcoatl legend may be a creation of the conquest and early Colonial times and brought together Aztecs and conquistadors in a mutually comprehensible story. The gist of this story was that, for the Europeans, the Indians were a people from the Bible and already understood some aspects of Christianity and had a great man or god who promoted Christian values, thus making sense of the subsequent conversions by the missionaries.

This Quetzalcoatl was something of a fake, in the sense that he was supposed to be a major pre-Hispanic god but was actually mostly a colonial fabrication in pre-Hispanic style, but with Western meanings. Such a hybrid being was easier for Europeans to see as pre-Hispanic and so to admire, because it was closer to their own culture. By comparison, Tezcatlipoca, a genuinely Native deity in the story, was much harder of access. As a later discussion will show, it is the perhaps the unconscious purpose of fakes to bridge the gap between Western and Native cultures, and great fakes do a wonderful job of it. The Colonial persona of Quetzalcoatl was a great fake, and many have believed in its authenticity over the years down to the present. It's not just that Quetzalcoatl was believed to be authentic, he was selected more than any aspect of "Aztec" culture for admiration and analysis by the various writers. More questions were apparently asked about Quetzalcoatl than about any other mythic personage.

The Lost Tribes of Israel theory has led to the actual creation of a religion in Mormonism. Mormonism emerged in the early nineteenth century in an atmosphere of American optimism that the New World owed little to the Old and was a special creation. Between 1821 and 1827 in Upstate in New York, Joseph Smith claimed to have received a new revelation from an angel called Moroni and written on golden plates that had been buried. He translated the text on the plates, written in late Egyptian, and published it as The Book of Mormon in 1830. The translation required the help of special stones called Urim and Thummim. The plates were so potent that they could only be seen by a few people for fear of death, and after the translation they were taken back to "heaven." Clearly the gold plates with their hieroglyphic inscriptions suggest Mexican civilization.

The Book of Mormon is the revelation of a chosen people who were the Lost Tribes of Israel and after the destruction of Jerusalem went into the wilderness and built boats that landed them in Mesoamerica. In Mesoamerica they built all the great pyramids and monuments and were, in fact, the pre-Columbian Indians. In The Book of Mormon they are referred to as the Jaredites. A subsequent group divided into two, the Nephites and Lamanites, who were in a bitter war with each other. The Lamanites were "evil." The group predating the Nephites, called the Jaredites, were Indians whose dates go back prior to 500 BC. Mounds in northern New York State, supposedly related to the ones in Mexico, were

Jaredite works and one of the places where the golden plates were said to be located. Because the Lamanites eventually destroyed the Nephites, the plates were buried for safety by Moroni, until they were found by Joseph Smith.

Besides wars among themselves, one of the main things that happened to the Mormons in Mesoamerica was that they encountered Christ and became Christians. This Christ was apparently a version of Quetzalcoatl. Christ is mentioned in most of the chapters of The Book of Mormon. He is supposed to have appeared in the Americas following his crucifixion and ascension. Because in the early nineteenth century there was little available specific information about the ruins and sculptures of Mexico, the references to ancient works are necessarily vague in The Book of Mormon, which is largely mythic and poetic.

Nevertheless, because of their Mesoamerican past, Mormons are very interested in Mesoamerican archaeology and history and conduct excavations and write scientific papers. They do not require that these papers have a Mormon point of view, believing that any information is ultimately to the benefit of the Mormon faith. Books are also written about Mesoamerica with a Mormon audience in mind, in which Quetzalcoatl, "the fair god," figures prominently as a version of Christ. The well-known relief of the Temple of the Cross at Palenque is mentioned as a forerunner of the Christian cross or the ancient Near Eastern symbol of the Tree of Life. (Von Däniken also referred to this relief as a "cross.") The Maya relief does represent a tree in the center of the universe that can be considered a Tree of Life, while it is also a "crossroads of the four directions," so it lends itself to such Christian interpretations.

The story in The Book of Mormon has been ridiculed by some scholars and laymen alike. There were dozens of books from the sixteenth to the nineteenth century that tried to explain the ancient Americans as the Lost Tribes of Israel, and there were even some books that might have served as the prototypes of The Book of Mormon. The Lost Tribes of Israel theory was to last at least until the end of the nineteenth century. It is not surprising that The Book of Mormon deals with that subject. What is surprising is that The Book of Mormon tries to reconcile the Bible and its world with the great cultures of the New World in one great sweep of narrative. Recent DNA studies have shown that American Indians have no genetic ties to the Jews or any other peoples in the Near East. This is a challenge to Mormons on a scientific basis.

Americans born here in a Christian culture could, like most congregations, have continued to look back to the Near East for religious inspiration. By contrast Mormons were trying to integrate the Old and the New Worlds on a mythic level in a more global story. Mormonism is technically an American religion, but it is also American in spirit, not just in place. Perhaps the integration did not work completely; Joseph Smith's text sounds too nineteenth century and not biblical enough, and mostly the racial and ethnic ideas on which the Lost Tribes theory rests had stopped being compelling for many in the twentieth century, but that does not take away from this interesting cultural attempt to come to terms with the Natives of America in religion.

That this project of integration has still not been accomplished is indicated by the current "alien" theory, according to which the monuments of ancient America were built by aliens. Paradoxically, we feel closer to aliens—who are after all our creations—than to the surviving Indians, who are robbed of their ability to have created their own civilization. Anthropologists are particularly upset by this stealth usurpation of Indian culture for the credit of other peoples. But it may be an attempt to find at least an imaginary common ground that may seem not to be there in reality. European Americans feel that Indians were more like us than both Jews and aliens, and we keep trying.

# V

# SUNKEN CONTINENTS

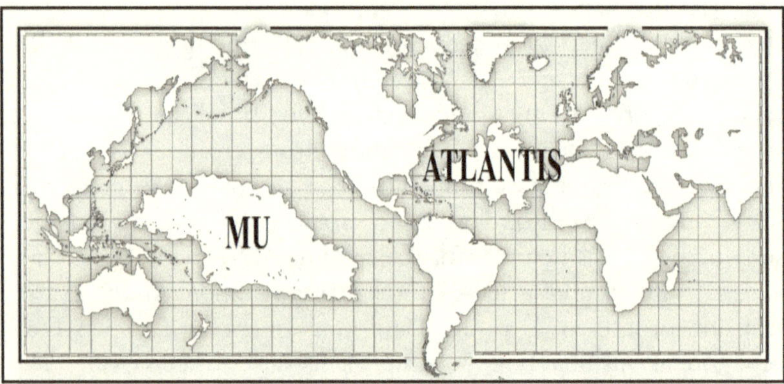


Fig. 4. World map showing the location of the imaginary continent of Atlantis between Eurasia and the eastern coast of the Americas, and the continent of Mu beneath the Pacific ocean.

For many people at the end of the nineteenth century and the beginning of the twentieth, theories of sunken continents accounted for the perceived similarities among ancient cultures, especially those of the New World. The continent of Atlantis was supposed to have been between Europe and America, and Mu (aka Lemuria) was supposed to have existed in the Pacific. Both were believed to have been destroyed in a great, sudden volcanic eruption and flood and sank beneath the seas 10,000 to 50,000 BC. The biblical flood was seen as the mythic memory of the cataclysm that destroyed the continents. Their ideas, customs and arts were believed to have had been spread to their colonies outside Atlantis and Mu proper, and thus some of their aspects have survived to our times.

The story of Atlantis came first and was inspired by a passage in Plato that describes an ideal world outside the Pillars of Hercules, near the western end of the Mediterranean, that was suddenly destroyed by a great calamity. It is now believed that something like that may have been based on a story of an eruption near Cyprus in ancient times. Plato's story may have been a dramatic and embroidered version of the Santorini disaster, as it was handed down by word-of-mouth tales. Mu was inspired by Atlantis, and by the scientific study of the distribution of lemurs, according to Darwinian concepts of evolution and dispersal.

Ignatius Donnelly, a colorful politician from Minnesota, known both for his uprightness and corruption, wrote the most important book on Atlantis, *Atlantis: The Antediluvian World*, which first appeared in 1882 and has been reprinted ever since. James Churchward wrote several Mu books, starting with *The Lost Continent of Mu* in 1926, and was especially popular between the two World Wars. While to the specialist these theories were completely off the wall, for a while they made a crazy kind of sense to their followers that is worth exploring.

The science of geology had demonstrated by the nineteenth century that lands had undergone great uplift and subsidence in the past, and the world had had a different appearance, so that continents in what is now ocean were entirely possible. Islands such as the Azores were supposed to be the not-quite-submerged mountain peaks of Atlantis. Moreover, geologists had already mapped some of the ocean floor to know that it was uneven, like a landmass. The news of entire islands being destroyed in volcanic eruptions fueled the idea of the possible destruction of continents, although there had not been a known precedent for such a colossal and instantaneous calamity, which was perhaps the most unbelievable part of the theory.

As in the theory of aliens, the scientific information was the necessary background for the ideas, but the ideas came from a different source. The concept of sunken continents died in the later twentieth century with the understanding of plate tectonics and continental drift. It is now accepted that the continents have in fact drifted over millennia and that the Americas and the Old World formed one single, huge landmass at one time. However, these movements were slow rather than cataclysmic and are not over. The continents are still moving. Geologically speaking, there is now no room for two more continents between the ones we know.

By the end of the nineteenth century and the early twentieth, much more was known about ancient America than in the sixteenth to early nineteenth century. There were thorough travelers' accounts exploring every nook and cranny and even some scientific archaeological excavation indicating with greater precision the monuments of pre-Hispanic times. These could be compared in detail to the monuments of the Old World.

Donnelly's book was illustrated with quite correct renditions of pyramids and sculptures that he had found in other books. He foregrounded in particular the late nineteenth century's favorite building with its elegant mosaic fretwork at Mitla. Mitla is a palace in the modern state of Mexico. Both inside and outside, the walls are covered with exquisitely fitted stone mosaic of designs such as stepped frets and diamonds. It has been appreciated for the precision of cutting, with stone tools, and the dramatic lights and shadow in the tropical sun. Mitla is now dated to about 1300 AD. Other structures with stone mosaics exist in the Yucatán peninsula, but Mitla was known earlier and is geometrically the most accurate. In Donnelly's book, the Mitla building is quite recognizable, even though the mosaic designs are schematic. He compares them to a Hindu building at Sarnath.

Despite all this knowledge of detail, the understanding of the Americas was still incoherent from a global point of view. People were still trying to figure out where the American civilizations fit in the general scheme of things. In fact, most of Churchward's and Donnelly's theories are concerned with the Americas and how they are like or unlike the Old World. It can be said that Westerners conquered the Americas, but they had not digested American culture and history. Atlantis and Mu were new attempts at creating a global synthesis. Their logic is quite clear; rather than imagining great migrations of the Lost Tribes of Israel or Egyptians from Europe to the Americas across improbably dangerous ocean journeys, they imagined an intermediate continent from which both the New and Old World cultures came. The logical benefit of the theory of those continents was that they contained in one place as a point of origin all the features of civilization found scattered all over the world and "explained" the similarities and diversities. It was a simple and practical theory, which however happens not to be true. Civilizations, alas, did not emerge in such a convenient way. Aliens have now replaced Atlantis as a popular theory, but sunken continents must have been a satisfying idea for their followers in their time.

Atlantis and Mu were imagined as Edens in a very biblical sense and as the motherland and fatherland of all humanity. There is a utopian strand in all the writings inherited from Plato's description. Plato described Atlantis as a supremely organized place, with a king and ten leaders controlling the population of agriculturalists and craftsmen. The lands were subdivided into equal sizes, and canals were used for irrigation and transportation. Plato's view of this "perfection" was quite regimented and perhaps even totalitarian. He did envision war and taxation for the military. All those who admired his Atlantis admired a place of calm and order unlike the messy worlds we know. Everything after Atlantis has been seen as a pale shadow or degeneration of the original. Moreover, believers in Atlantis and Mu imagine civilization created only once, to spread in imperfect form in the rest of the world. This single origin of humanity and civilization is the most striking and satisfying aspect of the sunken-continent theory.

The concept of Lemuria is of scientific origin and the name was coined in 1864 by a zoologist who was puzzled that that the fossils of lemurs existed in Madagascar, in India, and Indonesia, but not in the Middle East or Africa, in between. At that time scientists often thought that there were submerged land masses or bridges to account for such strange distributions. Philip Sclater proposed that there once might have been a connecting land between Madagascar and India. According to modern theory, Madagascar and India were part of an original land mass that broke apart, with continental drift—there was nothing between them that sank. On the model of a lost continent between Madagascar and India, there was supposed to have been another continent under the Pacific, also called Lemuria, or Mu for short.

James Churchward was an engineer and inventor who published *The Lost Continent of Mu, the Motherland of Men* at the age of seventy-five in 1926. Churchward claimed that his knowledge of Mu came from an Indian priest who disclosed ancient tablets from Mu, which he translated, more or less as in the case of The Book of Mormon. In actuality, Churchward probably knew of Mu from various other writers, in particular the famous spiritualist Madame Helena Blavatsky. She claimed in the 1880s that Indian seers known as the Mahatmas had shown her a book written prior to Atlantis, in which she read about Lemuria for the first time. For her the ancient Lemurians were bestial and mindless, and for this reason they were destroyed by God. She believed in multiple creations of the human race. Churchward turned these very imperfect Lemurians into a perfect race and made modern humanity imperfect both in spirituality and science by comparison.

As in the case of Atlantis, the universality of Mu was "proved" largely by ancient American monuments, artifacts and symbols which were similar to those of the Old World. According to him, the Lemurians wrote their numbers as the ancient Maya did, with a dot for one and a bar for five. Churchward's concern was spiritual—he saw Mu not just as technologically superior to our times but in religious terms. To him the heritage of Mu signified a religion of love, exemplified by the sages of all the current religions, especially Jesus. The ancients of Mu never feared God; they loved him with simple confidence.

The followers of both Atlantis and Mu were dissatisfied with their real civilizations and searched for answers in the mythical past. As Churchward bitterly ended one of his books, *The Sacred Symbols of Mu*, with the line, "Once again I ask—what is to be the end of this present civilization?" he was expressing a despair about his own world seemingly bent on self-destruction.

One of the lessons of popular visions of ancient America is that they are and were based on the science of their times but that they also expressed hopes and fears not allowed in the scientific literature. As ancient America was and is a popular mystery, it is a fertile place for these ideas to be played out.

# VI

# RACIAL MIGRATIONS

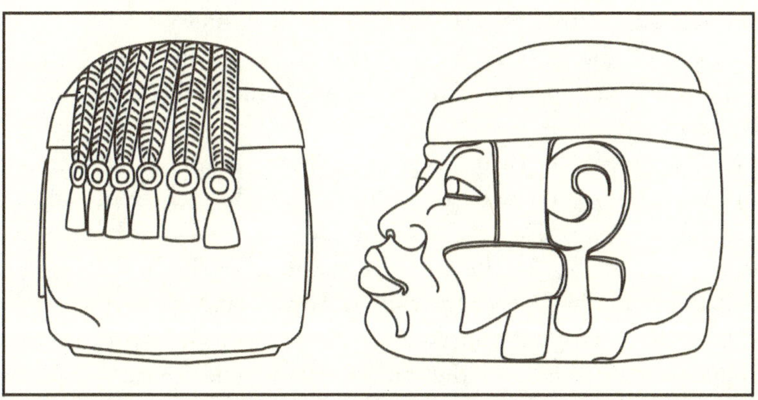

Fig. 5. Colossal Olmec stone head from Tres Zapotes, Mexico, c. 800 BC. The "African" facial features and the hairstyle reminiscent of cornrowing are supposed African features.

America was always believed to have been populated by immigrants; the question was only where they came from and when. Science places the development of modern humans in Africa, and all peoples in the world now are believed to have migrated ultimately from Africa. Such an origin was not clear for earlier centuries, but the Indians were nevertheless generally supposed to have come from somewhere else. This was due in part to the racial variety of the "red man." Unlike Whites, Blacks, and Asians, American Indians do not have such strikingly different racial characteristics from the other races. Moreover, depending on the person and tribe, they sometimes have features that are reminiscent of Whites, Jews, Blacks, and Asians, separately and together, thus making almost any theory of origin on a visual racial basis possible or impossible. Representations of facial features in clay, wood and stone have been used as "proof" of one racial identity or another. The twentieth century scholar Alexander von Wuthenau was the most holistic—he wrote a book about the clay figurines of Mexico and claimed to see all the human races represented in them (1970). To Wuthenau, the Americas were a great melting pot before Columbus discovered the continent.

In the nineteenth century "races" and "ethnic" groups were more or less equivalent concepts, thus defining Jews as a "race." There was a strong belief in the superiority of the White race and the inferiority of the others, and writings suggested the "obvious" and "necessary" hegemony of the White race over the others. Those who wrote books and looked into the subject of the Indians found much to admire and proposed origins that were relatively high in Western estimation. Thus the theory of the Lost Tribes of Israel proposed the Jews, who, while not as "great" as the White Christians, lived among them in a symbiotic relationship.

Non-Jewish "Caucasians" (a problematic term no longer in technical use) were also proposed as Indians, though less frequently. The Medievalist architect Eugène Viollet-le-Duc wrote an important essay for Désiré Charnay's book, *Cités et ruines américaines* (1863), on Mesoamerican architecture. He had never traveled in Mexico and wrote the book on the basis of Charnay's photographs. He was much impressed by the architecture of Mitla and the similar Maya buildings in the Yucatán peninsula, with mosaic ornamentation. But what interested him mostly was that the stone buildings looked as if they had wooden prototypes—wooden beams with trellis walls and columns translated into stone. Some buildings looked as if a thatched hut had been rethought and translated into limestone. He was aware of the fact that there were Hindu Indian temples that imitated wooden constructions, and he himself had argued that the great Gothic cathedrals of Europe had wooden prototypes. Viollet-le-Duc therefore thought that stone architecture with wooden prototypes was "Aryan" in origin and that therefore the American Indians had to have been Aryans.

The concept of "Aryans" was a mixture of a linguistic and racial category. It had been demonstrated that most of the European languages were related to each other and to Iranian and Hindu Indian languages, which coincided with what were described as "Caucasian" physical types and the creators of "superior" civilizations. This discovery of the Indo-European language family occurred in the nineteenth century. Being Aryan was about the highest compliment that could have been paid to Native American art and architecture. Viollet-le-Duc posited the idea that blond and blue-eyed Indo-European-speaking Norsemen came over to the Atlantic shores of America and made their way to Mexico.

A characteristic of early writers was that they imagined a migrating horde from a specific point, all racially and linguistically homogeneous, who arrived at their destination in a short time with little change in their way of life. One of the unusual aspects of Viollet-le-Duc's theory that the Indians were Aryans was that it was not based on facial features but on a mode of thinking through architecture. Most other writers were much more interested in biological features in determining Indian origins.

The person most fascinated by racial migration theories was Harold S. Gladwin, a well-to-do amateur anthropologist who had his own ethnographic museum in Arizona. His theories opposed the scientific establishment, which he tried to demolish through humor and ridicule. For example, he accused the establishment anthropologists of sleeping with their doors and windows bolted so that no new idea could ever get in. Gladwin's book, *Men out of Asia* (1947), brought together many of the earlier piecemeal migration theories in what he felt was a grand synthesis. Despite some very questionable assertions, there are interesting ideas in it, and it is worth a read. Gladwin followed the German Kulturkreis school of anthropology that believed migrations left behind remnants, like the rings of water after a stone had been thrown into a pond, in the order in which they occurred. That is, the earliest migrants lived on the very edges of the world and later migrants lived more in the centers. He thus posited that the earliest migrants in the New World were dark, perhaps Negroid people like the Australian Aborigines, who were later absorbed into other races but accounted for the Negroid characteristics to be found among the American Indians. Subsequently he posited a major "Mongoloid" migration into North America, which basically everyone accepts (though the term is no longer in technical use), since Native Americans have the straight dark hair, eye fold, and often the "Mongoloid spot." (The Mongoloid spot is a dark area near the bottom of the spine in Mongoloid babies that is later outgrown.)

The wildest aspect of Gladwin's theory was that after Alexander the Great's death in 323 BC, Mediterranean conquests in the Near East and India ceased; his army disbanded, and many of the men took to ships in search of new worlds to conquer and reached America. Alexander's army was a multiethnic and polyglot group, and on arriving in the Americas they would have brought "Caucasians" and other racial types with them. Gladwin attributed the rise of civilization in Mexico and Peru to their arrival. This made sense to him in 1947, because in the nineteen forties the depth of American civilization was unknown, and 300 BC seemed to be a reasonable starting point for it.

Now we consider New World civilization to have begun about 2500 to 1500 BC at the latest, and Alexander's ships could have had nothing to do with it. One of the problems in studying the ancient Americas is that the chronology is still fluid. Many sites are not dated with absolute certainty and can change by several hundred years back or forward with new research. Any theory that is based on the exact correspondence of dates is in trouble. It is characteristic of Gladwin and other adventurous theorists that they take the scientific data of their times for granted as the absolute truth and build on it—even if they rail against scientific information in general. Thus, as the effects of any Alexandrian migration seemed believable in the 1940s, the theory is totally untenable today.

Having brought Aborigines, "Mongoloids," assorted "Caucasians," and Asian people to the New World, Gladwin then imagined a migration of Polynesians to South America and the Caribbean. The Polynesians are well-known sailors who have spread from Hawaii to New Zealand to Easter Island over enormous distances. They had seagoing canoes and used currents and stars in navigation. Similarities in the languages of all Polynesian speakers indicate that they were related and only relatively recently separated from one another. Most mysteriously, the sweet potato, which originates in the Andes, is also a staple food in Polynesia and has the same name—kumara. This suggested to many that Andeans and Polynesians had to have been in contact. Similarities have also been seen between the Easter Island heads and Andean carvings. In Gladwin's view, the Polynesians came to the Andes and blended their sort of "Caucasoid-like," light-skinned race with the people already there. (For Thor Heyerdahl, who was also impressed by Polynesian-Andean parallels, it was the Andeans who went to Polynesia.)

Recently, a chicken bone was found in Chile in a deposit about a hundred years before European contact; its DNA indicates parallels specifically with Polynesian chickens. Spanish accounts refer to chickens in Inca Peru; before the DNA evidence, chickens had always been thought to have been an early postconquest introduction. The chicken is not a native bird in the New World, and now there is a suggestion that it was of Polynesian origin and that there was preconquest contact between Peru and Polynesia.

Reading Harold Gladwin, it would seem that almost every race and ethnic group came to the Americas and made up the Indian population. In this theory, the arrival of Europeans was just another racial migration to American shores. The fact that Europeans brought Africans with them just completes the global racial melting pot that was already there.

From the time the colossal Olmec heads, dating to before 1000 BC, were found in Mexico in the early part of the twentieth century, they were considered Negroid in features. Their wide faces, thick lips and heavy noses were seen as African physical characteristics. Strangely, not all Olmec art has such features—the faces on many of the jades look more Asiatic. Gladwin attributed such "African" features to an early migration of Australian Aborigine, Melanesian people mixed in with the others. More recently, Ivan van Sertima has written books researched in detail about the possibility of Africans going to the New World on their own. In *African Presence in Early America* (1987), the various authors consider old maps, histories, and linguistics, besides the colossal heads in constructing a hypothesis that the early Olmec culture was African inspired. Their theory is that the Olmecs came from West Africa at a very early time, c. 3000 BC or before, and were responsible for writing systems, the calendar, and even the languages in Mesoamerica. Some designs on Olmec heads remind writers such as von Sertima of specific details such as cornrowing hairdos found mainly in Africa.

The desire to attribute the origins of Mesoamerican civilization to Africans has a motive in racial pride—so much has been written about African slavery at the hands of Europeans, which many Blacks consider a humiliating time in their history, that they had a desire to be the founders of a great civilization and would rather contemplate their past as Olmec. As van Sertima writes, "My concern was with the reconstruction of those aspects of African ancestral history which transcend and redeem that later colonial chapter of debasement and humiliation (p. 6)."

There is no question that representations of people in pre-Columbian art suggest a variety of races and that we have no good explanation of the Negroid features of the colossal heads. The study of the racial identity of Native Americans is not an objective pastime and has a lot to offer or take away from certain groups. Modern Native Americans watch these theories with a some alarm. If their primacy in the New World is questioned, it affects their legal, moral, and other practical rights. There was a great deal of furor over Kennewick Man, discovered in Kennewick, Washington, in 1996, in layers beneath Native American skulls. The skeletal remains of Kennewick Man are thought to be "Caucasoid," Polynesian, or Ainu (of Hokkaido). Were these people here before the Indians? Many such theories assume that the "migrations" were of homogeneous peoples, rather than individuals of various types.

Current scientific hypotheses hold that Native Americans migrated to the New World across the Bering Sea at the time of the last major ice age, when there was a broad land bridge between the two continents.

They followed the large Pleistocene mammals, such as the mammoths and sloths, as specialized hunters. As they were nomads, they followed the animals and spread out relatively quickly throughout the lands, occupying both North and South America. Their spear points, known as Clovis, have been found in many places. The people who came from northern Asia were mostly an early version of the Asian racial family, although some members of other races could have been mixed with them. The biological differences seen among Native Americans are attributed to later developments in the Americas. It is believed that after the land bridge disappeared, there were no more major migrations to the New World. American anthropologists believe that there were no other migrations of significance to the New World from the Old and that the population developed in isolation. (There was one clear later migration of the Asian Inuit, formerly "Eskimo," but that was restricted to the Arctic area.)

Modern DNA studies are confirming a small but significant contact with Oceania, which could have happened before, after, or concurrently with the migration from Siberia.

The large animal fauna died out by about 8000 to 6000 BC, and Native Americans settled down, hunting smaller animals and exploring vegetable foods. This led to the domestication of plants by 4000 BC and the beginning of farming life and permanent settlements. These plants include many that we have adopted, such as maize, potato, sweet potato, tomato, chili peppers, beans, squash, and cacao, for a short list. Political developments such as powerful chiefdoms began by around 2000 BC and were manifested in grandiose architecture and sculpture in Mexico and Peru. States began to emerge by 1 AD, and empires conquered large areas by 1300–1400 AD in Mexico and Peru. For various geographic reasons Mexico and Peru were the most auspicious for the development of high civilization. Other areas of the Americas, such as North America and the Amazon, had more scattered populations and less of a concentration of monuments and cities, due to their geographic openness. The scientific story of the history of the New World is one of independent development, after major early migrations. Many have asked, however, why couldn't a people who once arrived in the New World not have come again and again, and why could they not have come by boat rather than by land?

# VII

## SEAGOING CRAFT

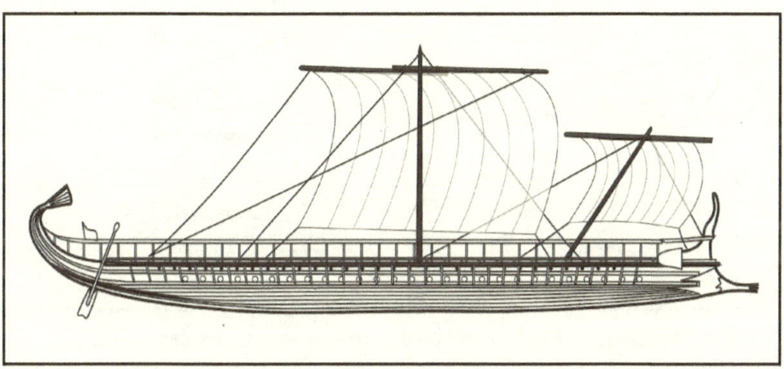

Fig. 6. Classical period trireme. A warship with many rowers was used by the Greeks and Romans.

Were there boats in ancient times that could have brought immigrants to the New World? The answer is a resounding yes. There were the Mediterranean triremes, the Chinese junks, the Polynesian outrigger canoes, and the Viking ships.

Perhaps the least seaworthy but possible boats were the warships of Greeks, Romans and Phoenicians, indeed before and after the time of Alexander the Great, as Gladwin imagined it. The triremes had three levels of rowers (often slaves), up to a total of several hundred, and a sail and were very fast. A large number of people could sail in a trireme, mostly warriors in Classical times. As warships, they were intended for relatively local battles and not for open-sea exploration or trade. While they might have crossed an ocean, there is no evidence that they did.

However, the Chinese junk could have easily crossed the ocean. The "junk" is not a pejorative term but a corruption of the Indonesian word "jong," which referred to these impressive ships. Junks had three, five, sometimes more sails and were the most advanced ships of their time in the world. Their origin was in the Han period, c. 1 AD, and they lasted

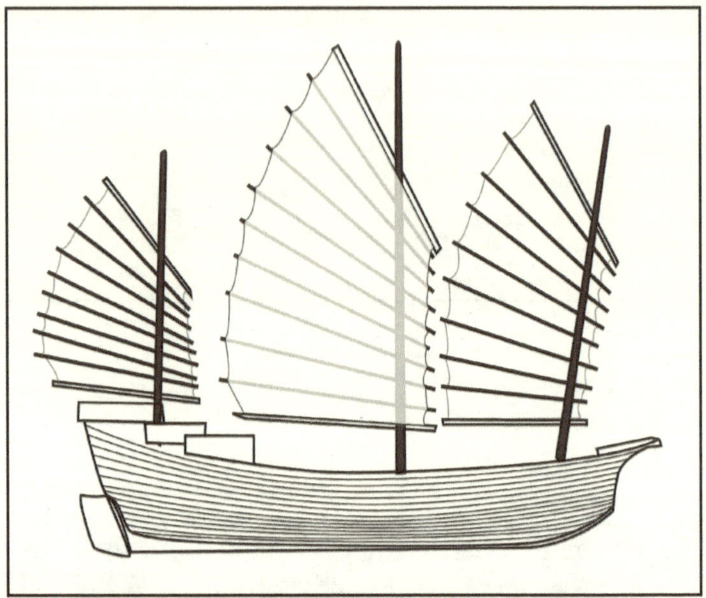

Fig. 7. Chinese junk. A large sailing vessel with several masts sailed throughout South Asia and perhaps into the Atlantic.

until modern, Western ships took their place in the nineteenth century. Smaller versions of them existed earlier. They were mainly trading vessels and came from China to as far as the Indian Ocean, through the island straits of Indonesia. There is an Italian account recorded in 1421, referring to Chinese junks possibly crossing the Atlantic and beyond. In a recent book, *1421: The Year China Discovered America* (2003), Gavin Menzies argues that a Chinese fleet led by admiral Zheng not only crossed the Atlantic but explored North and South America, as well as Australia. Chinese sources refer to Indian ships with seven sails carrying over five hundred persons and huge amounts of merchandise.

In about 400 AD a Chinese Buddhist devotee described a journey from Ceylon to Java in a Chinese junk manned by several hundred sailors and merchants, which was much larger than European ships of even Columbus's time a thousand years later. There is no question that the Chinese junks were adequate for a journey across either the Atlantic or the Pacific at an early time period. The question is, did they have a reason to go there?

Some Chinese sources refer to an emperor, Qin Shi Huang, who outfitted ships with food and water and sent them on a journey of exploration to a mythical land in search of the "elixir of immortality."

Others have suggested that groups of Buddhists went in search of new lands when they were expelled from their homelands in religious schisms. Curiosity and the search for exotic goods—as in the case of Columbus—are certainly not ruled out in the Chinese case. The conclusion is that Chinese junks could have come to the Americas and could have had the motivations to do so.

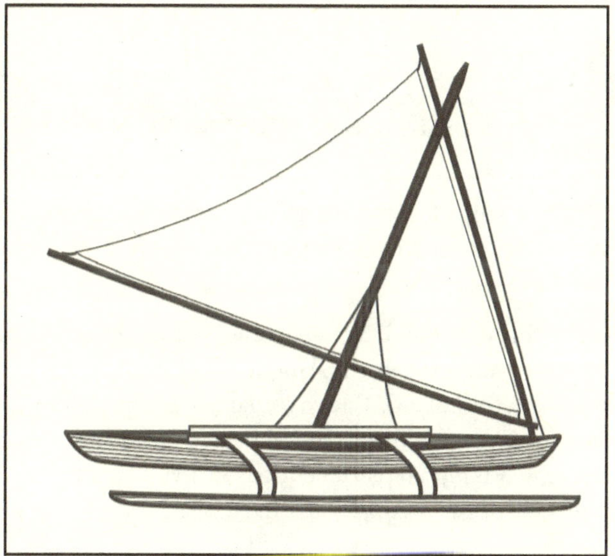

Fig. 8. Polynesian outrigger canoe. Canoes with stabilizing outriggers were used among the Polynesian islanders to go on voyages of thousands of miles.

Much simpler than the junk, the Oceanic outrigger canoe was also a seaworthy craft. The outrigger is a wooden plank that floats and parallels one or both sides of the canoe and creates great speeds and balance. Such outrigger canoes in Polynesia had sails and often a small cabin. Polynesian navigation by charts and by the stars is famous for covering enormous distances and colonizing most of the islands of the Pacific. Polynesian navigation consisted not just of accidental one-way journeys but of the ability to go back and forth among island groups. Going from Easter Island to the Andean coast might not have been that difficult. The dispersion of the sweet potato and possibly the chicken indicates Polynesian contact.

While the Viking ships were later, eighth to eleventh century AD, they

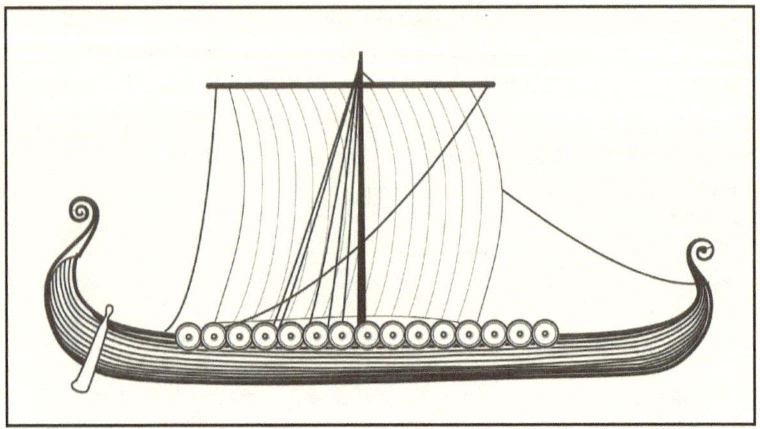

Fig. 9. Viking ship. Gracefully curved craft with rowers and a sail traveled as far as North America.

are relevant in this discussion because one Norse sailor, Lief Ericson, is believed to have sailed to North America and even to have founded a settlement in Newfoundland. Viking remains have been found on the tip if Newfoundland associated with the ruins of L'Anse aux Meadows. Like the triremes, the Viking ships depended on many rowers and had one large sail. Several actual Viking ships have been found archaeologically,

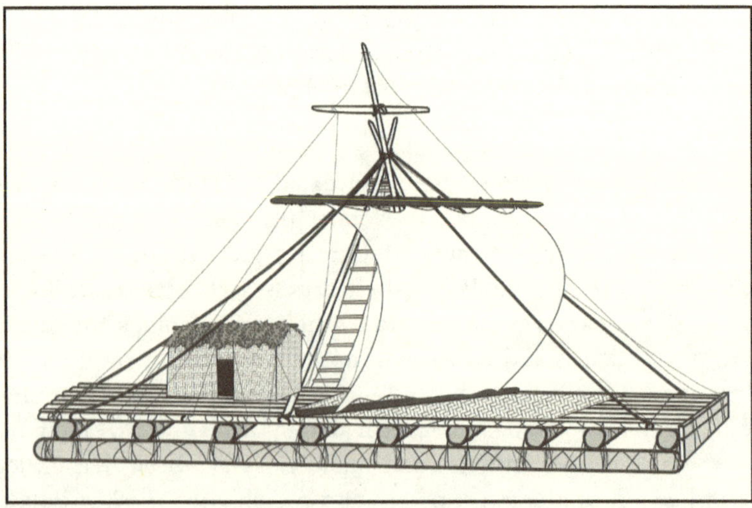

Fig. 10. *Kon-Tiki.* Thor Heyerdahl's balsa wood raft in which he sailed from Peru to the Tuamotu Islands in Polynesia.

so we know their construction in detail. They were light, watertight craft with elegantly curving prows and bows, carrying a hundred or so individuals. Their purpose was largely raiding, and they were mainly outfitted for warfare.

Thor Heyerdahl, a charismatic Norwegian amateur anthropologist and archaeologist, singlehandedly added two more types of boats that could have the crossed the Atlantic and/or the Pacific: the seagoing raft and the reed boat. Heyerdahl was interested particularly in Polynesia and did field research on the Marquesas Islands, which was eventually published as *Fatu-Hiva: Back to Nature* (1974), at the height of the counterculture in the 1970s, when he was a hero. He had read about Spanish reports of encountering large merchant rafts in the sixteenth century between Central and South America and decided to build a raft ship. Familiar with the arguments about Peruvian and Polynesian contacts and the case of the sweet potato in both areas, he was interested in finding out whether such a raft could make it from Peru to Polynesia. The rafts were built from balsa logs and were equipped with sails. A structure was built on top. Balsa wood is native to Central and South America, and while a hardwood it is remarkably light and buoyant. Heyerdahl named his

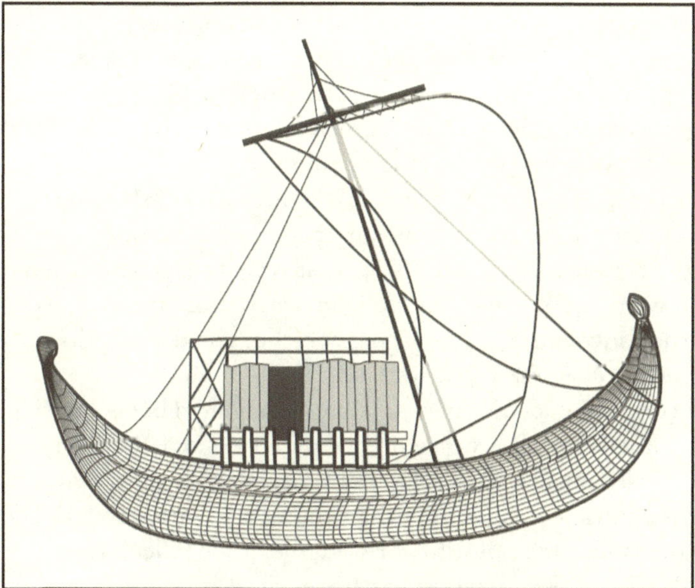

Fig. 11. The *Ra*. Thor Heyerdahl's reed ship in which he sailed from Morocco to Barbados in the Caribbean.

raft *Kon-Tiki*, after one of the names of the Inca god Viracocha. The *Kon-Tiki* raft sailed from Peru in 1947 and the westerly winds took it to the Tuamotu islands in Polynesia, in vindication of his theory. His book about the adventure was translated into fifty languages, and the documentary film earned him an Academy Award.

About twenty years later, Heyerdahl built another oceangoing boat based on a primitive design and unexpected materials. Small boats made out of reeds are known in Africa in the Lake Chad region, as well as in Peru and Bolivia. Heyerdahl wanted to test the idea of whether ancient Egyptians could have come to the New World in a papyrus boat. This boat was named after the Egyptian sun god Ra. Built on reconfigured ancient models, *Ra* was constructed by men from lake Chad, who were used to making reed boats. Launched from Morocco, the boat sank soon thereafter. *Ra II* was built by boatmen from Lake Titicaca in Bolivia, another reed-boat-building area, and this second version sailed successfully from Morocco to Barbados in the Caribbean. Heyerdahl built a third reed boat named the *Tigris* to prove Mesopotamian and Indian connections. All these boats and journeys have been subsequently made by others, indicating that they were not one-time successes but possible ways to travel.

Besides trying to prove certain routes and connections between ancient peoples, which did not necessarily work out, Heyerdahl ultimately did prove that great ocean voyages were possible with simple craft. Given the ships available in different cultures prior to 1492, plenty of ocean voyages were possible in ancient times. All of the ships discussed could have undertaken intentional long ocean voyages.

There are also accounts of modest boats, such as fishing boats, having been driven off course and ending up far away. According to Western records, between 1775 and 1875, in all twenty Japanese fishing junks were driven ashore in the Americas, anywhere from the northwest Coast to Mexico, involuntarily. If any got back, they could testify that there was land on the other side of the ocean.

In conclusion, people may have moved about in boats and ships a lot more in the past than we give them credit for. The issue is not so much whether they made it across an ocean, but whether their arrival resulted in any significant act involving the cultures they encountered. Did such immigrants become powerful, or were they soon killed? Were they seen as gods? Being seen as gods was the equivalent of being an "alien"—someone powerful, who absolutely did not belong and must have come from outer space. Did the immigrants alter the course of Native history?

Could a boatload of Africans, Chinese or Polynesians have much of an impact on populous cultures?

There are two important facts to be considered in these questions. One is that no imported object from any other part of the world has ever been found in the Americas in a scientific excavation (except possibly a chicken bone). Not a single Chinese coin or Sumerian tablet has come to light in excavations. Second, however, is the fact that the Aztec empire was conquered by a handful of men, mostly from one ship, with a superior military technology, with horses, and with the self-destructive Native belief that they might be gods. A technologically superior culture with the desire for conquest, treasure and land apparently did not have to have many men to create havoc in Native American society.

Isolated events similar to Cortez's conquests, of adventurers coming by boat across the Pacific, are therefore not impossible. Nevertheless, even if there were any, they may also have fizzled out like the Viking settlements. Getting a boat across is just the beginning of the problems in trans-Pacific contacts.

# VIII

## THE ASIATIC TIGER

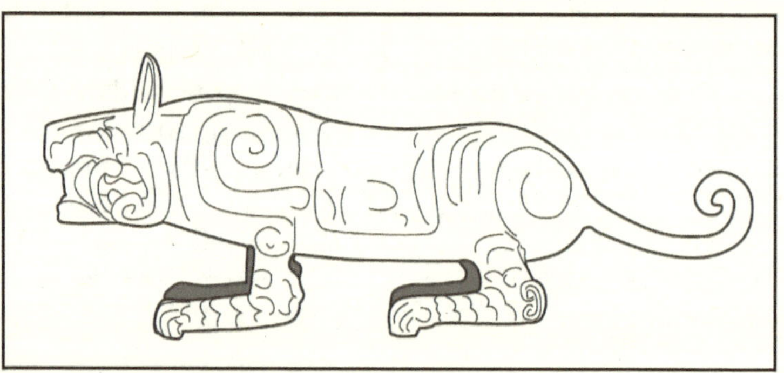

Fig. 12. Chou Period bronze tiger at the Freer Gallery of Art, Washington, DC.

In 1959 the highly respected Viennese scholar Robert von Heine-Geldern published an article entitled, "Representations of the Asiatic Tiger in the Art of the Chavín Culture: A Proof of Early Contacts Between China and Peru." This appeared in an academic publication, *The Acts of the International Congress of Americanists*, in 1959. Von Heine-Geldern was struck by the fact that the Andean jaguar image was shown with the stripes of a tiger, characteristic of Asia, rather than the spots of the New World jaguar, and he attributed Chavín art to transpacific contacts. Going beyond the strangeness of representing an Asiatic feline instead of an American one, he noted that the stripes on the Chavín image were done the same way as on the Chinese one, with two flat arcs meeting in a V shape. He was particularly impressed by this in comparing a Chavín mortar in Philadelphia to a Zhou period Chinese bronze jaguar. Besides the stripes, both have scrolls indicating feline pelt markings. The eighth century date of the Zhou bronze tallied well with the Chavín date as defined at that time. This specific parallel von Heine-Geldern saw as proof of transpacific contact.

From the 1950s to about the 1970s, in the academic community

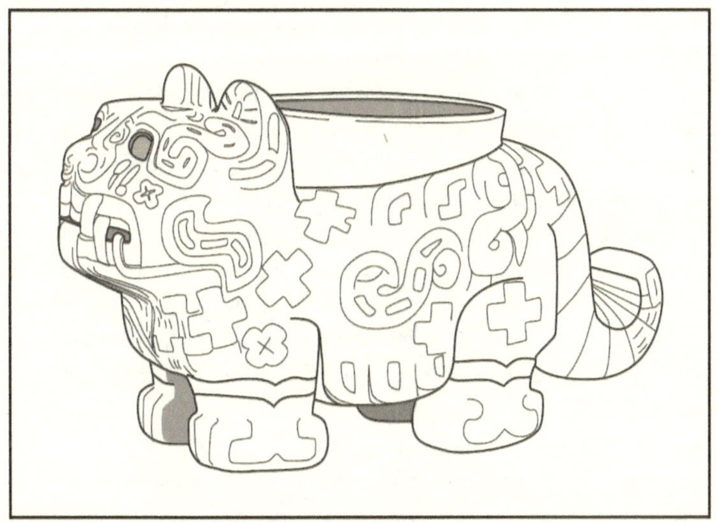

Fig. 13. Chavin style stone mortar from Peru at the University of Pennsylvania Museum of Archaeology and Anthropology.

there was a great deal of serious interest in the possibility of transpacific contacts. While some scholars always thought of it as "slumming," others were willing to consider the matter. A gate shut in the 1980s, and since then all such discussion has ceased.

Those interested in global interaction were called "diffusionists," since they assumed that people and ideas diffused over a large area. The opposition believed in "independent invention" and "convergence"—in similar things being created by similar processes in widely separated places. The diffusionists were accused of not giving the Indians credit for having created their own civilization and accused them of being anti-Indian. The "independent inventionists" were accused of myopia and not seeing the whole world as one interconnected system. For twenty years or more, these issues were debated in books, journals, and conferences. Now, the independent inventionists have won the day, since the diffusionists have been unable to close their case. It is now as impossible for a scholar of ancient America to study diffusion as it is to accept Atlantis or alien spaceships.

Von Heine-Geldern was the most distinguished of the diffusionists, with an impeccable background in the study of Indonesia. As a Viennese, he did not have to march to the same drumbeat American anthropologists followed. Many of his ideas and parallels were mentioned in earlier studies, but he systematized them and made them intellectually compelling. Von Heine-Geldern believed that there were two periods of intense contacts between the Americas and Asia: Chinese contacts intermittently between c. 900 BC to after 200 AD and Hindu-Buddhist contacts from about the sixth to the tenth century. He hypothesized that small groups of Asians must have settled among the Native Americans, while there was also traffic back and forth. He deduced their presence from similarities in their works of art. Unlike the vague similarities other writers found, von Heine-Geldern's parallels were detailed and specific. One had to see it in images, not evoked in words, and his articles were illustrated.

Chinese influence was seen from the Zhou to Han periods and was mainly centered on specific scroll and interlace designs. The Chinese examples were mainly on Zhou period bronzes and jades, while the Mesoamerican ones were on things like the marble vessels of Honduras or the ball-game imagery and paraphernalia of El Tajín. Similarities were also seen between Han period pottery and the covered pottery vessels of Teotihuacán. Mesoamerican pyrite mirrors were compared to Han bronze mirrors. Some of these similarities are indeed striking, especially in drawings where the context of the materials and size don't matter. Can similarity of development account for the structure of Mesoamerican and Chinese scrollwork? And if it does, why does it not occur elsewhere?

Hindu-Buddhist influence was seen by von Heine-Geldern as arriving after the Chinese, and he hypothesized that for various political

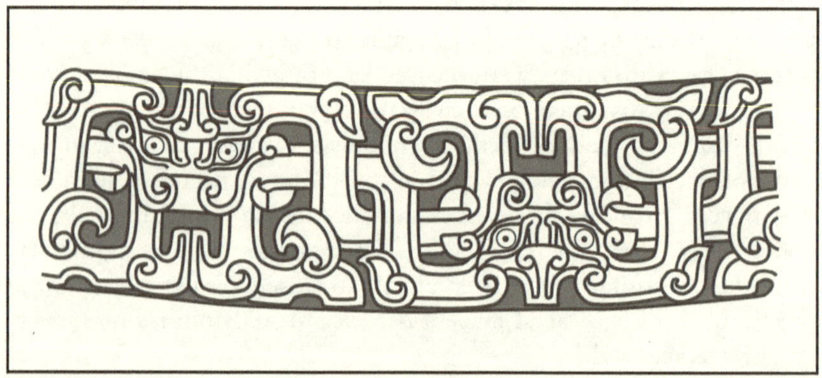

Fig. 14. Scroll design from a Chinese bronze vessel of the Chou period c. 500 BC.

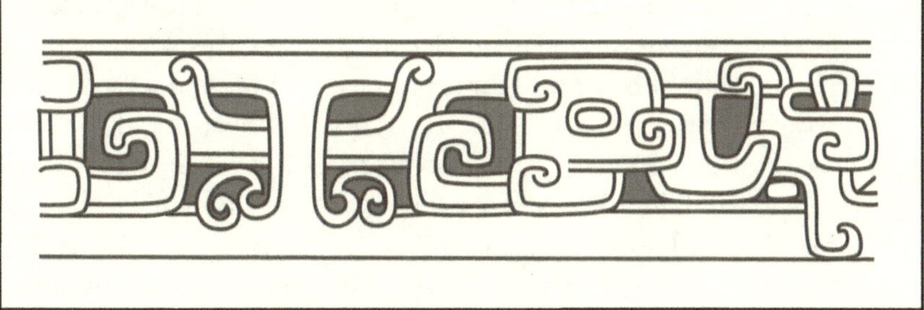

Fig. 15. Scroll design from El Tajín stone relief in Mexico, c. 1000 AD.

and economic reasons Chinese voyages ceased at a certain point, and Southeast Asian ones followed in their wake, probably with the help of earlier Chinese-derived charts and maps. These Hindu-Buddhist parallels are limited exclusively to the Maya.

Von Heine-Geldern was not the first to see Hindu influences on

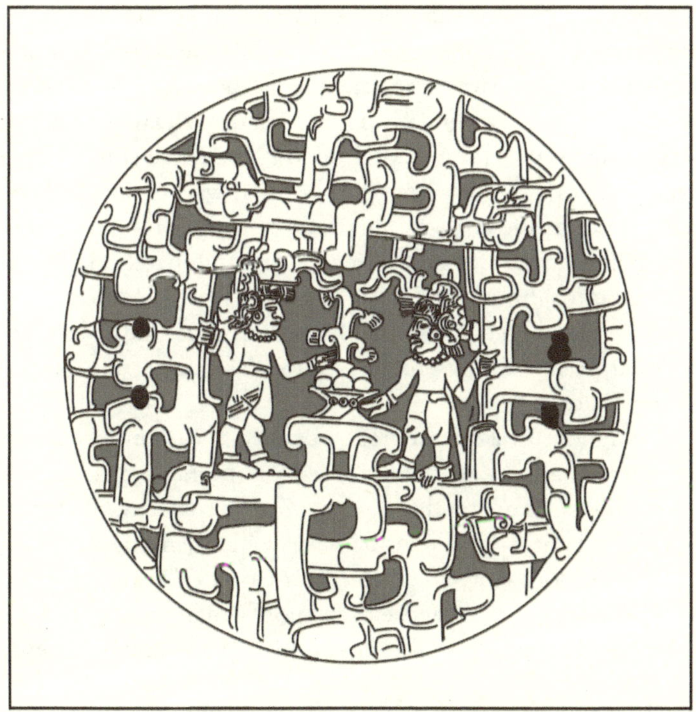

Fig. 16. Scroll design from a slate mirror back from Kaminaljuyu, Guatemala, c. 500 AD.

the Maya. Nineteenth-century travelers like Jean-Frédéric Waldeck saw a parallel between the sinuous and elegant Maya figures, such as those of Palenque, with Hindu and Khmer representation. Waldeck went so far as to misread parrot figures in art as elephant heads, and elephant heads were imagined in the ornaments at several Maya sites. Elephants meant obviously Hindus to Europeans. There are no elephants in the New World. Von Heine-Geldern was too sober to see elephants, but he saw trunk-like upper lips as derived from Indian makara-monster representations in art. But he was most impressed by the half-cross-legged poses and casually leaning figures of Palenque rulers, which to him were reminiscent of Indian Buddhist figures. The famous Temple of the Cross relief of Palenque, favorite of the nineteenth-century theorists as a "Christian symbol," he now compared to Cambodian and Balinese examples of the Tree of Life. The design of reclining figures holding a lotus vine at Chichén Itzá was compared to a similar design from Amaravati in India.

Besides point-by-point comparisons in art, von Heine-Geldern saw parallels in cosmology—such as the five creations of the universe in Mesoamerican belief compared to the multiple creations of India—and the calendar. The Mesoamerican calendar has been extensively compared to Chinese and Indian calendars, more recently by David Kelley as well, and they all agree that these complicated systems are somehow related, though no one quite knows how they got that way. As has been pointed out many times in the last few hundred years, the Mesoamerican board game of patolli is very close to the Indian game parchesi. There is no known reason for this similarity.

When I entered graduate school in the late 1960s, diffusionist studies were at their peak, and my professor, Douglas Fraser, was a disciple of von Heine-Geldern.

In preparation for a conference to be held at Columbia University in 1967, Fraser organized an exhibition of photographs with a catalogue written by his students, entitled, *Early Chinese Art and the Pacific Basin.* Fraser's idea was first of all that there was Chinese influence all over the Pacific, from Indonesia to the Northwest Coast of America, not just in Mexico and Peru. He selected eleven motifs that existed in the art of early China and found those throughout the Pacific region. These were:

- a long tongue;
- an architectural mask;
- a displayed (legs spread) monster;

- a displayed figure with flanking figures;
- a double-headed serpent (Sisiutl) figure;
- an alter ego (an animal over the head of a figure);
- monster mask headgear;
- a simultaneous image (two profile images that can be read as a single face);
- a knife blade that looks like a tongue;
- a rump mask;
- a forehead lozenge.

Fraser argued that where there was one of these images there were usually two or more of the others, indicating that these motifs spread as a complex. Monster faces were the basis of at least half of his list, and they were presumably inspired by the *t'ao t'ieh* monster masks on Shang and Zhou bronzes, whose meanings are obscure to us. Fraser asked his students to research these motifs in their area of expertise but not to theorize about Chinese contact, which he did himself. I wrote six of the essays, one on the displayed flanked figure among the Maori, one on the alter ego in Mesoamerica and Central America, and one on the simultaneous image in Mesoamerica, of which there were a lot, and assorted others. Each section in the catalogue began with a Chinese example.

Did we believe that these images were indications of Chinese influence? I don't think that any of us believed it wholeheartedly, and none of us went on to study these issues in our later scholarly lives. At the same time, we suspended disbelief and explored these exciting new ideas with enthusiasm—maybe there was something in them. Fraser himself abandoned this approach and in the years that remained to him, before his early death, turned to a more conservative study of African art.

Another distinguished New York scholar interested in diffusion was Gordon Ekholm, the curator of Mesoamerica at the American Museum of Natural History. I also studied with Ekholm at Columbia University. He was particularly interested in the Hindu-Buddhist-Maya parallels and was a firm believer in ancient people's ability to move around much more than was generally accepted.

The archaeologists Betty J. Meggers and Clifford Evans believed that even the craft of pottery in the New World had been introduced from Asia around 3000 to 2000 BC. The finds of Valdivia in Ecuador were the earliest pottery known at the time of the discovery and were too sophisticated, technically and in form, to be a beginning tradition; Meggars and Evans saw similarities with the pottery of Jomon Japan. They suggested that accidental voyages from Japan brought the technique of pottery making to the New World from Asia. The earliest pottery traditions in the New World are found on the Pacific Coast of the Americas, from Ecuador to Mexico, and may be connected to an origin near Valdivia.

By the later 1970s diffusionist explorations shut down in academia, leaving a vacuum that von Däniken was to fill with his "chariots of the gods" and "aliens" published in the 1970s. For von Heine-Geldern, Douglas Fraser, and Gordon Ekholm, the aliens were the Chinese and the Hindus, who had become comfortably integrated into the pre-Columbian and Pacific cultures.

As I go over the heritage of my graduate-student days, I am impressed by the fact that this line of inquiry died out, but the issues, in particular with China, have not disappeared. There have been many excavations of the pre-Xia-Shang period in China with the discovery of fantastic jades and pottery. Quite a number of people have mentioned to me how pre-Columbian it all looks and whether there is explanation for it. I have to agree that there is a pre-Columbian feel to many of the pieces, but I have no idea how to explain it. Besides the new discoveries, what is striking in the works of von Heine-Geldern, Fraser, and Ekholm is that the parallels are restricted to two general and contiguous parts of the world. After all, pre-Columbian art does not look like African art, Egyptian art, or Greek art in any reasonable scholar's estimation. Most of the parallels are restricted to China—such as, for example, the love and veneration of jades in both cultures. But until that Chinese bronze coin is excavated in the Americas, this will remain only a curious theory.

# IX

## GREAT FAKES

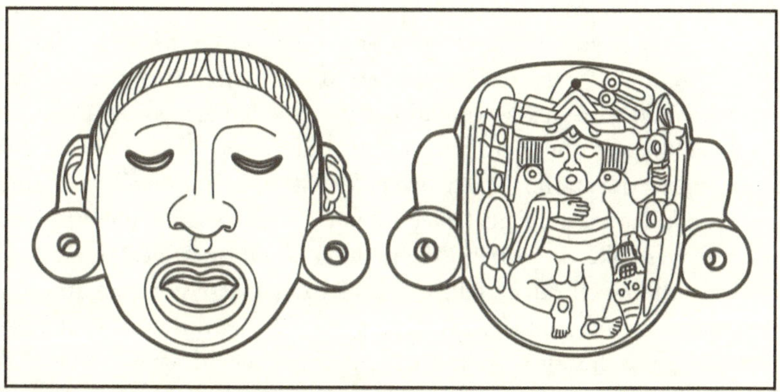

Fig. 17. Stone mask of the Aztec flayed god, Xipe. The back of the mask shows a four-armed dancing figure. The British Museum, London.

Fakes in ancient American art indicate the same confusion about Native identity that Indians have had in the Western imagination in writings. A fake is an object created by someone modern to look like an ancient work of art. It requires some familiarity with the style and subject of works in the past and the ability to reproduce them well enough to fool a buyer or collector. Making a fake requires entering the mindset of someone from another culture. In fact, however, as this is impossible to do completely, the faker actually has the mindset of his own culture's ideas about the past, rather than the past itself. His own culture is in the work. As long as certain ideas about the past are commonly accepted, the fake passes for the original quite successfully. But when the ideas about the past change, a fake is sometimes unmasked, because its modern aspects become visible. It begins to look more like a modern than an ancient work.

When the fake is accepted as an original, it works to embody an ancient culture the way texts like The Book of Mormon have done. Such works are focal points that crystallize thought and discussion. This is not to refer to ordinary faked souvenirs and modest forgeries meant to fool the traveler and small collector, which are pretty easily identified, but to great fakes that were meant to be sold to the most exacting collectors and/or their connoisseur advisers and are now mostly in museums. Some of these great fakes have been further selected by writers and scholars in publications as the best examples of the arts of their culture. It may take fifty to a hundred years for someone to notice that these hallowed objects are fakes, and even longer for everyone to accept it. Great fakes may still not have been unmasked and confuse our idea of what is original in a particular culture. Museums tend to remove fakes from view and from texts expeditiously, out of embarrassment that they have been taken in by them and out of a desire not to contaminate the rest of their collection. I think this is a mistake—fakes offer wonderful lessons in what we think and have thought pre-Columbian cultures and their arts were like. They tell us something about ourselves, the way von Däniken's theory of aliens tells us more about ourselves than about the pre-Columbian past. In a way, these great fakes are the illustrations to accompany the theories about Native Indians, which have exercised the Western imagination for so long. Three great fakes that have recently been unmasked are the Aztec ones, discussed below: the Xipe masks, the birth-giving goddess, and the crystal skulls.

In my early years of teaching, I used to keep two striking Aztec masks as masterpieces for my concluding remarks on Aztec style. They were frequently illustrated in books. The masks were especially beautiful because they had simple forms with elegant and refined details. Made of basalt, they were well polished with mongoloid eyes, a meditative expression, and beautifully carved striated hair. The tautness of the skin indicated that they were meant to be masks of the god Xipe, who was honored by a sacrificial victim, whose skin was flayed and then worn for a while by a priest in one of the most horrendous Aztec sacrifices. Beautiful as the image was, it was also grisly and thus presumably characteristic of the Aztecs.

Figures were carved in low relief on the backside of the masks, but at first I paid them little attention. The way the classroom was set up, I would talk standing in front of the screen, not actually seeing the slides I pretty much knew by heart. In 1978 I happened to turn around and actually took a careful look to explain to the students what was on the slide. I used my pointer to indicate the dancing figure, as I said, "In one hand he holds a shield and banner; in the second hand he holds a rattle staff . . ." And then I swallowed hard, "In the *third* hand he has an incense bag and . . . a bit of *drapery* is folded over the *fourth* hand across the chest." Ancient Mesoamerican art did not have figures with four arms—multiple arms and heads were characteristic of Hindu Indian art. Ancient Americans would have considered multiple arms monstrous. Ancient American art did not have drapery—cloth falling in folds—which was characteristic of Classical European art. I stood transfixed in that class, because I had just realized that my supreme examples of Aztec art must have been forgeries.

The mask I was showing was one of two similar ones in the British Museum. The main difference is that on one the mouth is carved out in a circular opening, while in the other it is closed. Adjustments were made in the back relief figures to fit in the available spaces. As one of the masks was in a British collection by 1861, if they were forgeries, they had to have been early to mid-nineteenth century forgeries. Could that have been possible? Research showed that there was a great deal of interest in the Aztecs and their art in the nineteenth century, both by Mexicans and by foreigners living and traveling in Mexico.

Jean Frederic Waldeck, the artist collector who imagined elephants in the arts of Palenque, originally started his trip in Mexico City and got interested in Aztec art. He and his expatriate friends were particularly interested in the flaying ritual of the Aztecs as the epitome of barbarism. Waldeck made several imaginary drawings of priests wearing flayed skin masks. Whoever made the British museum masks must have selected that subject to titillate those collectors and connoisseurs who were interested in flayed images. (The name of the deity Xipe had not yet been attached to these representations, and whether or not other Xipe sculptures are also forgeries is not clear.) Whoever made the masks was not terribly familiar with Aztec art and religion and thought it was similar to Hindu art in giving the back figure four arms. Other Asian features include the eyes and the delicate part in the striated hair reminiscent of Buddha figures. The maker of the masks was not necessarily aware of the specific Asiatic sources of these elements but was trying to make an exceptional, and probably expensive, work of exotic art. The general effect sought was the barbaric but refined, which was believed to be the characteristic of Aztec art. At this time many, including Waldeck, thought that the Indians were the Lost Tribes of Israel or Greeks or Hindus or any other ancient peoples, and a four-armed figure would not have seemed strange to them. It did not seem strange to most of my contemporaries.

These masks, at the time canonical works in the British Museum, were later copied to make newer fakes and inspired modern artists such as Henry Moore. They were published in most books on ancient American art. When I presented my doubts about them at a conference, the reaction was great disappointment. "You can't take them away from us," said several people. "We can't do without them." But since then, the masks have been removed from exhibit and from among the illustrations in books without detriment to the Aztecs or to us. They now belong to a segment of history no one is much interested in. Once unmasked, fakes tend to disappear.

A great fake is not only better than the originals, it is more like the arts we are used to and like. The Asian features of the British Museum masks were like the theories of the Lost Tribes of Israel, or like the "Aryans," or the Asians in the many migration myths about the Native Americans. In all cases, the actual Native American and his things were not great enough without the combination with another great culture for our admiration. In the case of the masks, the admirers of them were self-admiring their own artistic values more than the culture of the Aztecs. One can go further and posit the idea that the Aztecs and other ancient Americans could best be admired through such hybrid intermediaries as the Colonial Quetzalcoatl, Atlantis, and the British Museum masks. Every era seems to have its own manufactured intermediaries, which are unmasked only many years after their manufacture. The era for which they were made cannot see them as false.

While analyzing the striated hair on the British Museum masks, I unavoidably compared them to a sculpture in the Dumbarton Oaks Collection in Washington, DC, which was one of the most famous pieces of pre-Columbian art—the so-called Tlazolteotl, or birth-giving goddess. Made out of a greenish stone, it represents a naked woman giving birth to a child emerging from her middle. The figure is shown in a strange pose, squatting with her hands on her back, and the head and two arms of the child emerging between her knees. Her head is thrown back, her face contorted in a wide grin, presumably of pain, and her hair falls in neat rows down her back. There are no such graphic representations in Aztec art; there are even very few naked women. The closest parallel is a page from the Codex Borbonicus, which dates from the early Colonial period. As that figure has been identified as Tlazolteotl, that name has also been given to the Dumbarton Oaks birth-giving goddess. Tlazolteotl, literally the "eater of filth," was the goddess to whom people confessed their sins. Since sins could be confessed only once in a lifetime, people waited until late in life to confess them. Like baptism, the confession of sins was another one of the seemingly Christian practices of the Aztecs the missionaries were interested in. In the Codex Borbonicus, the goddess gives birth to a miniature version of herself, suggesting some kind of theological or metaphoric meaning we are not sure of. In the sculpture, there are no symbolic elements, only a woman giving birth to a genderless child.

Acquired in 1947 by Robert Bliss, whose collection formed the basis of the Dumbarton Oaks museum, the birth-giving goddess became one of the most famous pieces of pre-Columbian art, published in many books and articles to raves about its form and subject.. At the museum, it was the piece most sought after and visited by the public. It was admired for the virtuosity of the cutting of the hard, greenish stone—generally believed to be jade—for the universal theme of the mother and child, and for the representation of pain in its face and body, presumably characteristic of Aztec sensibility. The sculpture was bizarre and comfortingly everyday at the same time.

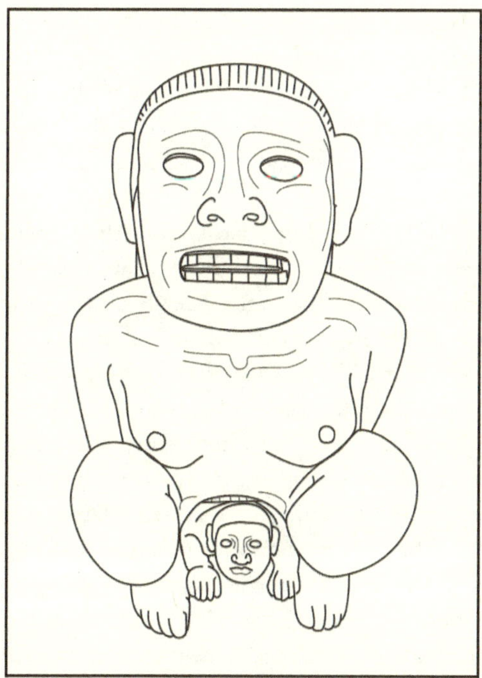

Fig. 18. Greenstone birthgiving goddess, Dumbarton Oaks, Washington, DC.

As a graduate student, I already knew in the 1960s that Gordon Ekholm of the American Museum of Natural History thought that it was a fake, and his assessment made immediate sense to me. When I asked him how he knew, he said it was the parallel lines of the hair, which could have been done only by mechanical cutting instruments and not by pre-Columbian tools. In those days, Gordon Ekholm was *the* arbiter of what was and was not fake in the Mesoamerican field. Most new pieces in private and dealers' collections went across his desk. However, most scholars of ancient American art preferred to think that it was not just genuine but a masterpiece, and that Ekholm was the oddity.

The striations in the hair of the masks in the British Museum seemed strange to me from the beginning, since no documented figures had such hair. They were also so similar to the striations of the hair of the birth-giving goddess, and in view of Gordon Ekholm's opinion, I felt that it too was probably a fake. I presented the British Museum masks at a Dumbarton Oaks conference, but I was dissuaded from calling the birth-giving goddess a fake in print—by museum personnel, who were most vocally against my doing so and argued that I presented no proof that that piece was fake, and as it was genuine by the acclamation of scholars in general I should desist from doing so. As I had done no specialized research on that sculpture, I acceded to their wishes in the publication but continued to regard the image as a fake. I did not include it in my otherwise comprehensive book on Aztec art, as an indication. (*Aztec Art* 1983)

In 2000 I organized a conference at the Metropolitan Museum of Art, entitled "West by Nonwest," where I was interested in exploring the idea that through pre-Columbian art we really end up studying ourselves. Again, I listed the birth-giving goddess among other questionable pieces in ancient American art. There was still a debate about its authenticity, but the idea that it was fake was no longer considered outlandish. The talk I gave, "Truth in Forgery," was how fakes may be untrue about the times and places they are supposed to be from, but they are quite true about us—about what we think of the Aztec, Maya, or Inca at any given time. It is because they are true about ourselves that we are so attached to them and consider them masterpieces.

In 1981 Steven Spielberg created the first Indiana Jones movie, *Raiders of the Lost Ark*, about an adventurous archaeologist of an earlier less-scientific era of archaeology. Indiana's first adventure in a South American temple involved finding and stealing a gold idol. The idol was in the shape of the best-known, pre-Columbian work at the time, the birth-giving goddess from the Dumbarton Oaks collection, thus making that image familiar to millions.

Eventually, Dumbarton Oaks allowed and desired to find out the truth about their birth-giving-goddess sculpture, and they put it up for technical analysis. Jane Wash performed extensive microscopic and scanning examinations and in 2008 concluded that the sculpture was a fake. The material it is carved from is not jade but wernerite, something unused in pre-Columbian times. The carving was done with rotary tools and other jewelers' tools using diamonds and not with pre-Columbian tools. In particular, the straight lines of the hair could not have been done in ancient times. The image of the goddess, once so much a part of Dumbarton Oaks's identity, has been removed from their website, as if it had never existed, which is a shame, in that it tells an interesting story.

It is unclear where and when the sculpture was made and why. It was owned by private collectors and dealers prior to the Blisses, whose collection and estate became Dumbarton Oaks. Various legends grew up about its origin, all of which seem to be untrue. A well-known turn-of-the-century French dealer of fakes as well as original pieces, Eugene Boban, owned it. The sculpture was clearly intended to be a shocking masterpiece. It is now one of OUR works of art and history and should not disappear without explanation.

Skulls are one of the common motifs in ancient American art, and the more-than-a-dozen skulls carved from rock crystal have been of great interest to us in the West. They are either thought of as Aztec, because of the subject of death, or Maya, because one of the skulls was supposed to have been found at the Maya site of Lubaantun in modern Belize. Rock crystal is very hard to work with ancient tools, and the perfection of the carvings and the smooth polish have made these very special objects. There is one in the British Museum and one in the Paris Musée de l'Homme, but the largest and most elaborate one has been in private hands. The so-called Mitchell-Hedges skull is unique among crystal skulls in having been carved in two pieces—the jaw is separate from the rest of the head, although carved from the same piece of crystal. It is named after the archaeologist Albert Mitchell-Hedges, who excavated in Lubaantun in the 1920s. According to legend, very likely propagated by herself, the skull was found by his adopted daughter, Anna, under an altar at Lubaantun. Auction records reveal, however, that Mitchell-Hedges bought the skull from Sotheby's in London in 1943. Anna kept the skull in her own possession, sometimes exhibiting it for a fee. After her death, it went into the hands of her companion.

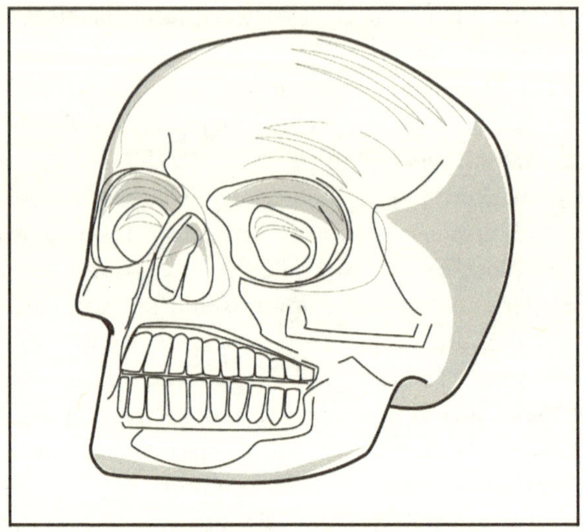

Fig. 19. Crystal skull.

The myths that have grown around the crystal skulls were perhaps begun by Anna Mitchell-Hedges, who claimed that when near her the skull told her of the secrets of Indian life and lore. In the same way that crystal balls are to predict the future and reveal the past in our own folklore, these abilities were transferred to the crystal skulls as well. The crystal skulls are believed to be benevolent and to heal, but, as skulls, they also have the potential to harm and to cause death. Most recently they have been associated with a legend attributed to India, that the Goddess of Death has thirteen crystal skulls which were intentionally kept apart. As there are more or less thirteen crystal skulls, depending on how they are counted, the number thirteen has become associated with them. There was a lot of speculation that, according to the ancient Maya calendar, an important four-hundred-year-old cycle (the *baktun*) would end in 2012, which might be a day of catastrophe, like the millennium dates in the Western calendar. One way to avoid that catastrophe was by bringing together all thirteen crystal skulls.

There are no securely dated crystal skulls in ancient American contexts. There is one famous Colonial example in which a small crystal skull is at the base of a cross. It is quite possible that, originally, the crystal skulls were meant to be Aztec early-Colonial relics. Jane Walsh, who analyzed the Dumbarton Oaks birth-giving goddess, had previously studied the crystal skulls, since the Smithsonian, where she works, had been given one as a gift.

She argued in 1997 that the only material that cuts crystal successfully is something of the hardness of diamonds, which were not available in Mesoamerica and that these skulls could not have been made in pre-Hispanic times. She finds the use of modern rotary tools in the manufacture of the skulls—which were developed at the end of the nineteenth century. Several skulls went through the questionable art dealer Eugene Boban. There is evidence that Boban acquired them from Germany and that they were probably made in Germany in the late nineteenth century.

Devotees of the skulls no longer argue for a pre-Hispanic origin. They note a strange feature of manufacture, which is that the skulls have been carved against the grain, which should not have been possible in either pre-Hispanic or modern times, because the crystal should have shattered. That alone is taken as an argument against the theory that the sculls are fakes. They argue that they were made by a sophisticated technology that we can't even imagine as yet. This super-technology is either placed by them in the most remote times of perfection, in Atlantis, or among extraterrestrial aliens. Dates for the skulls have been given anywhere from 5000 to 100,000 BC, following the Atlantis theory. Many now see the crystal skulls as belonging to a higher civilization that is perhaps yet to come from outer space.

Steven Spielberg, who seems to have a feel for ancient American fakes, picked up on the fascination with crystal skulls in his 2008 movie entitled, *Indiana Jones and the Kingdom of the Crystal Skull.* I have already mentioned that his ancient American inhabitants turn out to be extraterrestrials. They have crystal skulls that don't look anything like the existing ones. Presented as Maya rather than Aztec, the skulls have Maya-style artificially elongated heads. The story is based on the thirteen-skulls legend and is about returning one of the crystal skulls to its rightful owner, as a way to avert catastrophe. Once the skull is put in place, the aliens go.

Some objects are said to have intrinsic mystical power. Skulls are in themselves awesome and ambivalent images of life and death. There is something especially miraculous about the purity and translucency of rock crystal as a natural material. Skull and rock crystal together may be potent images for any culture but are particularly so for ours. The most successful fakes are the ones that arouse us to wonder about others as if they were ourselves—not the ones that really capture the genuine strangeness of another time and place. In fakes we admire ourselves through the mirror of another culture. Truly strange things are hard of access, and fakes, as long as they are unmasked, provide the role of intermediaries in the quest for understanding. So far, the crystal skulls have escaped the usual fate of disappearance from the scene, by finding themselves a new meaning in popular culture, and they may remain enigmatic objects for a long time to come.

# X

# THE QUESTION OF INDIAN IDENTITY

The identity of the ancient American Indian seems to raise ultimate questions about not just the history of humanity but about the universe itself. Six centuries after Columbus's voyage, which was epic mainly from a public-relations point of view, we still don't know where to classify Native Americans. We do not have this problem with White people, Africans, Chinese, Hindu Indians—who are quite clear to us, culturally and biologically. Interestingly, all of them have also been identified with Native Americans. Native Americans remain a mystery needing a solution. Native Americans have rarely been identified by anyone in academia as active agents in their own history—they are usually passive recipients of supposed foreign genes and inventions. Their existence is still such an anomaly that it calls into question religious issues about the nature of the universe and God's creation, and it's not surprising that at least two religions, Mormonism and Falun Gong, have been based on interpretations of Indian relics and history. In both cases, the antiquity and marvel of the monuments is said to account for another people's origins, annexing the Indian past to their own. It is possible to annex the Indian past to almost anyone, when it doesn't seem to belong to anyone. Ancient American ruins raise for many the question of whether there is a god at all, because, as things are, they make the world so complicated and unknowable. The existence of Native Americans raises questions about evolution and creationism. As the devotees of Atlantis and Mu indicate, we don't understand the universe until we understand the role of Native Americans in it. The scientific position of a migration across Bering

Straits is not satisfying to many, because it leaves the Indians isolated from the rest of humanity. Popular and some scientific sentiment wants to incorporate Indian history into world history, with the Lost Tribes of Israel or Chinese or Hindu merchants in transpacific contacts.

It has been said that there is a "scientific" and a "mystical" view of the Americas, the first of which is correct while the second is wrong. All these authors imagining a pre-Columbian melting pot are searching for something in world history that says more about their own time and place than about the Indian past. Many are searching for a place in the sun, to prove that their people did a major bit of discovery and culture building. Others are searching for a utopian Eden in the past. Some are searching for legitimacy in the New World. For most of them, the New World is a handful of famous monuments to be appropriated, the way Cortés and Pizarro appropriated the gold. To some extent all these theories are taking hold of the pre-Columbian treasure. But then so is the scientific establishment, and who is to say that the scientific establishment should have a monopoly of the Indian past? Moreover while the scientific establishment is not very good about communicating with the non-specialist person, populist theorists are bestsellers and make the public aware of the Indian past and its significance.

Populist theorists like science; it just isn't the science of anthropologists. Physics and geology have helped them to create elaborate scenarios for the Indian past. It is characteristic that most of these writers dislike modern civilization and prefer to live in their invented antiquity. So do many anthropologists; it's just that their antiquity is different, and for them the game is about scientific parameters to describe the "truth." Actually the populist theorists keep abreast of the current truths, such as dates and finds, but use them for their own purposes. So there is an orthodox establishment side by side with outsider theorists to explain ancient American identity for the general public. There is anger and mistrust between them and generally no interaction. The populists would like legitimacy and the scientists do not wish to recognize them and their issues.

The newest of the theories, most appropriate to our age, is the one about extraterrestrials. This theory is simply a modernization of the Lost Tribes of Israel and the Chinese exploration theories. With one fell swoop, the extraterrestrial theory explains religion and the gods as well. Mankind misunderstood the aliens and thought they were gods. The gods we know are therefore the aliens themselves. This theory attributes great power to the aliens, and the issue of power is writ into the populist accounts of ancient America. These aliens bring their culture, their technology, and teach it or force it on the Natives, with whom they presumably intermarry. The model for this interaction is the Spanish conquest, in which the conquistadors were taken to be gods, instituted their culture, and wed Native women, creating a hybrid race. On a more general level, it is also the story of English, French and Portuguese settlers in the New World. The populist writers are at pains to prove that such hybridity created ancient American civilization in antiquity, much as hybridity exists in the present. Anthropologists and Indians are invested by populists in the idea of isolation, who insist on their purity and uniqueness, until a single moment of encounter.

Fakes prove that behind the most authentic-seeming images lies hybridity. They demonstrate the fact that we don't really understand the artifacts of the ancient American past and tend to like works that are either caricatures of that past or that represent our own aesthetic and spiritual ideas about them. In admiring them, we are admiring ourselves, our own knowledge and taste. The fact that important fakes are not unmasked for fifty to a hundred years, or four or five generations, after they were created suggests that such hybrid images are potent representatives of an imagined ancient American culture, and we are unwilling to give them up easily. The scientific establishment which would not buy into the aliens theory has bought into the Xipe masks and the birth-giving goddess sculptures. It means that the scientific establishment is also not in full control of ancient American culture. That might also suggest that the populist theorists could also be occasionally right. Early people have moved about in the world far more adventurously than we give them credit for. Some contact would not destroy the independent development of ancient American culture. Some similarities, such as those with China, still beg for explanation. One need not close up the Indian in a diorama but find a place for him in global history. If the scientific community does not do it, moviemakers will.

Mel Gibson's 2007 *Apocalypto* was an ambitious attempt to recreate Maya culture on film, in a diorama. His characters even spoke the Yucatec dialect of Maya, which the moviegoer reads in subtitles. Most actors were Mexican of mixed Indian and Spanish blood. Maya specialist scholars were consulted about dress, jewelry, and architecture. Gibson's story is simple; the protagonist is a poor Maya man living in a thatched hut in a remote village. His existence with his family is idyllic. He and other villagers are captured by a band of warriors from the city and taken back to the city as slaves to be sacrificed on the temple pyramid. Due to an unexpected solar eclipse, he escapes the knife and runs away, followed by vicious warriors. Eventually he or the creatures of the jungle kill all the pursuers, and the hero escapes back home to his wife who has just given birth to their second child. There are various spectacular sequences in the film, but this in brief is the story.

Given all the authentic detail, what is striking is Mel Gibson's vision of the Maya—the most sophisticated culture in ancient America. To him the Maya are almost naked savages bristling with bizarre nose and ear ornaments and tattoos, reveling in violence. They reminded me of footage I've seen of New Guinea headhunters. Only a small part of the movie takes place in the city, where the only event is human sacrifice. Clearly Gibson preferred the lower-class hero and life in the thatched huts. To the anthropologist, the special features of the Maya are their complex writing and dating systems, their dynastic history, their fantastic architecture and beautiful sculpture, including the portraiture of an elegant, aristocratic elite. Nowhere is the film was there any aristocratic elegance. While the architecture of the set copied existing Maya architecture, it was crude in detail rather than refined. I did not recognize the Maya I knew from the monuments in the film.

This vision is not unique to *Apocalypto*. *Stargate*, which takes place in the ancient Egypt of the pyramids—supposedly built by extraterrestrial aliens—also glorifies the humble, homespun-wearing "slave" classes against the evil, artistic, and high-class ones. In our own mass entertainment through the media, the message is that the elite who created the ancient cultures were evil, and all their beautiful arts are tainted with that evil. Only the peasants are fine. This may be because film is a democratic medium and is meant to appeal to the "little guy" rather than to the wealthy. But we also make films about the rich in order to enjoy their wealth vicariously. Or, our heroes sometimes become rich. Such was not the story of *Apocalypto*.

At the end of the movie when the hero and his wife find each other and look through the trees, they see European ships in the sea, harbingers of the collapse of their world. The message seems to be that this horrible world will vanish, and no one should mind. While most of those who are nostalgic for the ancient American past imagine themselves as part of the artistic elite, the sixteenth-century story that the world of the Indians was conquered by righteous Europeans, because of the Indians' brutal excesses, is still with us. In Mel Gibson's vision, the moviegoer is to enjoy the reenactment of Maya brutality, with the assurance that Spanish ships are waiting in the wings. For Gibson, the ancient American is not associated with one of the world's high cultures but with savages. Sending out a movie like this reinforces for thousands a brutal vision of ancient America.

Mel Gibson's view is not unique. Recently I was a talking head on a National Geographic special, entitled *Pyramids of Fire*, about Teotihuacán, the Mexican site with the great pyramids, which I had worked on. There was little spectacular information on Teotihuacán that would please an audience, according to the moviemakers, so half way through the program they created a dramatization of a human sacrifice that took up the rest of the time. All Mesoamericans practiced human sacrifice, but Teotihuacán seemed more involved in representing water and fertility subjects, but these were of less fascination to the program's creators.

Human sacrifice is a complex subject, since it has been practiced in many places in the world, especially in ancient times, and needs a global explanation. What emphasis should be placed on it in ancient America? Suppose US histories began with the dropping of the atom bomb on Hiroshima and Nagasaki or included these facts in all of their presentations of American culture? Obviously, we place them in context, and we need to do the same in the New World.

Less interested in the theme of the "brutal ancient American," which was perhaps expected in a movie, most writers have been fascinated by the high civilization of the Americas and have attributed it to all other cultures of the globe and beyond, in disbelief that it could have been created by the Natives themselves unaided. The scientific community has no problem with this, since it believes in convergence. "Convergence" is a term that comes from evolutionary biology and means that similar environmental situations create similar biological results. For example, in order to exist in water all creatures need gills—whether they are fish or mammals like whales (which do not, a complication for convergence). Or, similarly, in order to have flight, creatures need wings, whether they are insects, birds or mammalian bats. Transferred to social theory, the argument is that when societies reach state-level development, they necessarily build great architecture, and the pyramids, such as those of Teotihuacán, were created to fulfill local political and economic situations and need not have been built by the Egyptians or the Jews.

Convergence has its own romance. If ancient America developed isolated from the Old World, it is a testing ground of how civilizations evolve. The mystery of ancient America is that it was a high civilization with a low technology. With some exceptions in South America, most of the Americas used stone tools for all their activities. In European terminology, they were Neolithic. Nothing so spectacular was done in the European Neolithic. On the other hand, ancient American social and political organization was far more sophisticated than anything in Europe, and marvels were created through organization.

We know more about the social and political organization of many North American groups than those of Mexico and Peru because they lasted into the nineteenth century and were extensively described while still functioning. The League of the Iroquois and of other Northeastern United States groups are thought by many historians to have influenced the political structure of the US. Bruce E. Johansen argues that the system of electing leaders and the federal structure of tribes suggested to men like Ben Franklin that similar forms be adopted. Most of the traits admired were forms of democracy and egalitarianism. This issue has been of so much interest among scholars that in 1996 an entire book was devoted just to the bibliography of the subject.

Parallels with the cultures of Mesoamerica and the Andes have been difficult to draw because, on the surface, those polities appear to be more absolutist kingdoms and empires. However, the Aztecs, about whom many sixteenth-century sources do exist, did elect their rulers. Dual rulership characterized the Aztecs and has been proposed for other Mesoamerican cultures. Moreover, the Aztec empire was a Triple Alliance between three cities and did not have territorial control over its subject states, requiring only tribute payments. Much is made of the fact that among the Aztecs and Inca, land was communally owned by family "clans" and could not be sold individually as in Europe, and thus could not be the basis of a capitalistic system. In much Mesoamerican imagery there is no emphasis on a supreme ruler, and "councilor" governments have been hypothesized as a check and balance on the ruler in major places like Teotihuacán and Chichén Itzá. The Maya kingdoms appear to be obsessively dynastic, according to their inscriptions, but they were small by comparison. The Inca empire was huge and territorial but with significant local autonomy. The Inca ruler was elected from within a large family. While political structures are hard to determine archaeologically, the very size and complexity of the sites, given the low level of technology, suggest organizations that were based more on consensus building than on the absolutism of force. William Brandon argues that New World societies tended to be more open and pluralistic, while Old World societies were more acquisitive, more closed, with a tendency toward absolutism and adversarialism.

It is hard to know to what extent the pre-Columbian cultures we know only archaeologically are now unconsciously judged to have been absolutist like the European ones on the basis of a general model. Certainly, wherever Europeans conquered they saw "chiefs" and "kings" and wanted to deal only with one individual for the sake of efficiency. There are many instances in which European traders literally created chieftaincies by focusing on and gifting a single leader selected by them. Brandon and Johansen suggest that in general American Indian social and political structures favored more participatory patterns than the European ones. I argue that this worked better for them in an environment of low technology and "explains" the marvels of architecture and sculpture that were created.

The ancient American example suggests, in the convergence model, that there is more than one way to create civilization. It also suggests, however, that in a general way cultures go through the same developments from the village to the state. There would be no way to know this if all we had were the civilizations of the Old World, which were all historically interconnected. Ancient America's isolation is necessary to understand how cultures evolve.

Older-generation writers always complained that ancient America did not have the wheel, which was to them a necessary item of civilization. Oddly, Mesoamericans had the wheel for clay figurines and toys or ritual objects but did not use the wheel for practical purposes. That's like complaining that China only invented gunpowder for fireworks and did not use it for guns. The wheel was of no use in Mesoamerica without draught animals on mountainous terrain. The point is that ancient Americans did fine without the wheel, and hence it was not necessary for the creation of their culture. The romance of the Americas is *low tech, high art.*

Since the time of Columbus, the West has been projecting its own ideas on Native Americans. What we project are our own hopes and fears, as much about ourselves as about the Indians. Adventurous, creative, or passive and primitive, these views are ours and say more about ourselves than about the Indians. Because ancient Americans are no longer with us and are unable to speak for themselves, we communicate with them through their monuments. Their works of art and architecture were made by their hands for their purposes and are our best insight into their minds. Of course, these works are also a matter of interpretation, but we honor their memory at least to have some idea of what they accomplished.

# XI

## WHAT ONE NEEDS TO KNOW ABOUT ANCIENT AMERICAN ART

The ancient Maya ruins of Tikal in Guatemala were the setting for the rebel headquarters of Luke Skywalker and Han Solo in the enormously popular movie, *Star Wars*, which began filming on location in 1976. In the sci-fi saga the ruins were said to be on the moon of the planet Yavin, somewhere in outer space. These steep pyramids emerging from the Central American jungle looked so exotic they did not resemble anything on earth. No way could monuments of the Old World—the Greek Acropolis, the Roman Colosseum, or even the Indian Taj Mahal—have been so used, because those would have been immediately recognized as historic sites belonging to certain specific times and peoples. In our imagination, ancient American ruins are unknown blanks and therefore can be "extraterrestrial," and it is not surprising that bestselling books have attributed them to aliens. We in the West don't know the ancient American monuments well enough to tell Tikal from Teotihuacán or Machu Picchu or even the Aztec from the Maya or Inca. The ancient American past is not taught in schools as the equivalent of the European past—it is not taught at all. Various scholars, usually of foreign origin, have complained that Americans do not know and teach the marvels of the ancient American past even though that is their proper antiquity.

America has always had strong bonds with Europe, rather than the Indian past. With its democratic government, the US has presented itself as being politically more advanced and superior to Europe and the rest of the world. Culturally, however, for some time Americans were considered to lag behind Europe, and well-to-do Americans have always made pilgrimages to the shrines of Europe to soak up culture. This changed only during the middle of the twentieth century, when both American mass and high culture were influential and admired worldwide. Nevertheless, America has always seen Europe as its privileged ancestor. The eighteenth century with its revival of Greek and Latin Classical antiquity, including its democratic and republican ideas, was literally foundational for the US.

The eighteenth century was also the time of the idea of the "noble savage," a heroic man of nature, based largely on Native Americans. The ancient Greeks were sometimes compared to Polynesians or Native Americans. But the idea of the noble savage was discussed more in the salons of Europe than in the US, because Americans were still at war with the Indians, in pursuit of territory. Jefferson wrote some fulsome lines about noble Indians but also had land conflicts in which he gave not an inch. Classical antiquity was conveniently dead and far away, whereas the red man was inconveniently close.

Only in the nineteenth century were the ancient American ruins available to those interested in exploration, in travel accounts and books. World Fairs and even the staged spectacles such as Wild West shows acquainted a larger group with Indians. Nevertheless, the conflict with Indians was not over, as they were being relentlessly pushed into reservations. Nor is this conflict over in the twenty-first century, despite millions of dollars being made in the gambling casinos by modern Indian tribes. A sovereignty movement exists on most reservations wanting to remove US government control even further. In Latin America, where most of the ancient American ruins are located, the Natives have either blended with Europeans or have become impoverished peasants with only a folk remnant of their former traditions. While the sixteenth-century conquest of the Aztecs by Cortés and of the Inca by Pizarro were sudden, spectacular, and mostly complete within a century, Indians in the rest of the Americas were being conquered in a long process for centuries and are often still controlled and/or protected today. The Indian may have been a charming and fascinating topic of conversation in Europe but is sometimes an uncomfortable subject in the Americas. There is no way that the US can see the Indian heritage as "ancestral" or uniquely in the sense of first arrivals in the land.

For a brief period in the middle of the nineteenth century, when the

US was developing the concept of Manifest Destiny and pushing its borders into its neighbors' territory, there was a concept of "America" controlling most of the continent, including the Indian ruins in Central America. Travelers like John Lloyd Stevens and archaeologists like Edward H. Thompson routinely "bought" ruins the way the US bought the Louisiana Purchase. This interest resulted in exploration, publication and public awareness of the great achievements of the ancient Americans. This interest has not lasted.

There are all too many reasons why ancient America would not be of immediate relevance to the US, except for harboring a handful of specialists and a few interested in exotica. Insofar as the Indian past shares the New World with the current European derived cultures, the geological proximity alone suggests the benefit of some acquaintance. Moreover, the monuments of ancient America are rich in artistry, in engineering and ideas, and those peoples communicate with us directly through the things they made. If we knew a little more about them, we would not have to resort to fantastic theories like the Lost Tribes of Israel or aliens from outer space. Or if our imaginations fancy those theories, we would have some information to compare them with. The imaginative theories prove that there is now a great unsatisfied interest in the public about the Indian past. Some Latin American countries such as Mexico have embraced their own specific past as a part of their national identity. The more powerful Anglo countries that have not so far might find value in future in accepting the significance of New World antiquity next to their Classical past in their educational systems.

In the pages that follow, I will list some of the major monuments of Mesoamerica and the Andes that everyone could be familiar with. There are many other possible lists created by others from different points of view. Mine is the result of many final undergraduate exams in which I hoped the students would go away from the course on pre-Columbian Art with the most important essentials. It is astonishing how many items on my list are there because we in the West selected them as most worthy of notice for our reasons. Some of these reasons include the issue of naturalism versus abstraction, which is a major theme in Western art history. The list also reflects what we in the West like, such as colossal stone monuments. To that extent the works of ancient America are already a part of Western history, and I merely suggest increasing the dialogue.

This is probably not the list ancient America might have selected, even if it had been in a universalizing mode. It is obvious that since most of these monuments have been accidentally or archaeologically discovered, we do not know what has been destroyed or missing. As in other parts of the world in antiquity, our knowledge is fragmentary, but it is a large fragment so that it is possible to generalize about it. Still, new spectacular works are found from time to time that might affect the list. Despite many recent advances, anthropological and historical understanding of these works is often limited or full of controversy. What follows is a basic list of the most important monuments of ancient America in Mesoamerica and the Andes that an interested person might want to know, with a brief commentary.

## MESOAMERICA

Mesoamerica was an area, like Europe, consisting of a number of separate cultures never completely united in a single empire, but always in commercial, political, and cultural contact. The area comprised southern Mexico, Guatemala, and Western Honduras. Here people lived in agricultural villages, making pottery and clay figurines by 3000 BC. The first powerful chiefdoms were those of the Olmec, in the pre-classic period, who began colossal earth architecture and stone monuments before 1000 BC in the isthmian region of Mexico. The most important Olmec sites are San Lorenzo, La Venta, and Tres Zapotes. Olmec art is surprisingly naturalistic, was ancestral to the later Mesoamerican traditions, and pieces were passed on as heirlooms—one jade mask was found in the Aztec Templo Mayor, deposited almost 2500 years later.

The period from 300 to 900 AD is considered the "classic" period, because that is the time when the Maya used dated inscriptions on their monuments. Of the hundreds of Maya sites in the jungles of Mexico and Guatemala, the most important are Tikal, Palenque, Yaxchilán, and Copán. The area was never united in a single empire but consisted of feuding and intermarrying principalities. The Maya are known for their beautiful and elegant depictions on monuments, focusing on their dynastic rulers. Earlier and contemporary with the Maya was the great city of Teotihuacán, whose ruins lie about an hour from Mexico City in an arid highland zone. Known for its colossal architecture, Teotihuacán is also unusual in not representing rulers and elites on its monuments. Teotihuacán may have had a trading and/or military empire. Major cultures also existed in Oaxaca at the site of Monte Albán and in Veracruz at the site of El Tajín.

When the great classic centers had collapsed by AD 900, they were followed by cities that imitated the earlier arts, such as the art of Tula and Chichén Itzá, in an eclectic fashion but preferred a more stylized rendering of images. Much image making was in the Mixteca-Puebla style, which combined Teotihuacán, Maya, Monte Albán, and El Tajín elements. The best surviving Mixtec works are books—or codices. The greatest empire of this post-classic period was that of the Aztecs, c. 1424–1521, with their capital, Tenochtitlan, located under present-day Mexico City. The empire did not include the former Maya area. The greatest artistic achievement of the Aztecs was stone sculpture in which they used themes from their history and mythology to aggrandize their rule. The Spanish conquest led by Hernán Cortés cut short the Aztec development. The Aztecs are known for their human sacrifices, but these were customary in the other cultures as well. All Mesoamericans shared a calendar system and a religious view of the gods sacrificing themselves for humanity, in return for which men had to make human sacrifices.

## THE AZTEC CALENDAR STONE

Perhaps the most famous monument from the New World, the Calendar Stone image is stamped on everything from ash trays to key chains and handbags in Mexico and is vaguely familiar to many. Its fascination for us is that it seems to encode the intellectual achievement of the Aztecs within its mysterious concentric circles and compartments. The Calendar Stone reveals the Aztecs as complex and civilized, capable of moving this 11.8-foot, 24-ton stone of hard basalt. Any culture that carves colossal stones with complicated images is admired in the West. Add to that the mystery of an ancient calendar and a glyphic system, and the monument's importance is not surprising.

The Calendar Stone was found in 1790 during repairs near the Cathedral of Mexico City, which had been the center of the Aztec capital city, Tenochtitlan. It was found with two other spectacular monuments, the "surrealistic" Serpent Skirt and the historical Stone of Tizoc. Since it did not appear to be an "idol," in the enlightened eighteenth century it was not destroyed and has been a symbol of the Aztecs ever since. It is a fragment, and its original location is unknown.

Some aspects of the Calendar Stone are very clear, some not clear at all. The most "calendrical" is a ring of symbols around the central image.

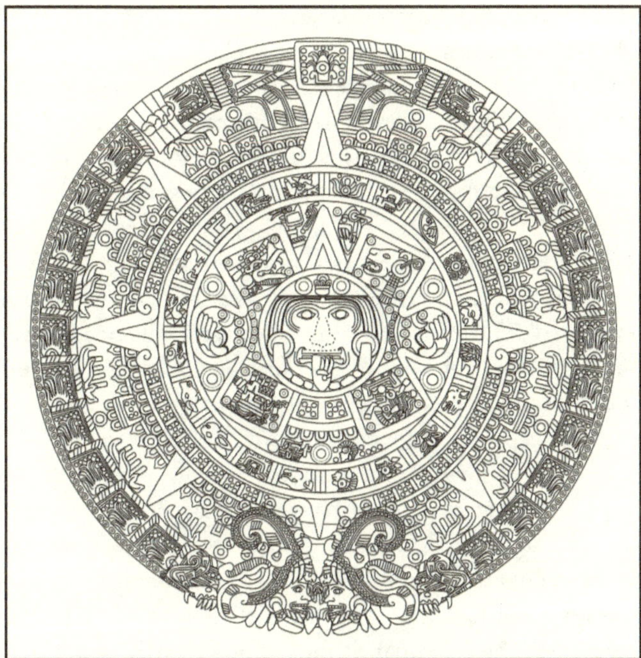

Fig. 20. The Aztec Calendar Stone.

In Mesoamerica such 20-day signs were combined with 13 numbers to form a 260-day divinatory cycle that in conjunction with a 365-day solar cycle formed a grand time period of 52 years. The Calendar Stone just shows the day signs and not the numerical permutations.

The central image shows a face with a long tongue and two clawed hands. It is surrounded by four squares with symbols and deities with four dots signifying the number four. These four squares represent the four previous creations of the world that had been destroyed by floods, fiery rain, jaguars, and wind, all on day four. The personage in the center represents the fifth world, which in turn will be destroyed by earthquake, for which the symbol is "four movement," the X-shape outlining the deity. The actual identity of this personage is unclear; some believe it is the sun, some the earth, some the sun in the earth or some other combination. With a few exceptions, Aztec deity identifications are problematic. In general it is clear that the stone represents the pessimistic cosmology of the Aztecs in terms of the great cycles of time in which humankind is a small player and does not appear except in a few small glyphs.

Several small dates are historical and refer to Montezuma II, to the year in which the Aztecs began their migration to greatness, and the date of their decisive conquest in the area. It is likely that the Calendar Stone was carved under Montezuma's reign (1501–1519). Several other dates, as well as the faces in the border serpent's maws, are as yet not clearly deciphered. As far as we can now tell, the monument demonstrated and glorified the Aztec support of the present cosmic era by rituals and sacrifices.

It is characteristic of Aztec state representation that it was not the rulers who were glorified by images, but the forces of the cosmos which the rulers served. The Aztec empire was a weak alliance between three cities in which the rulers were in no position to aggrandize themselves unduly. Their strategy was to represent the cosmos. The calendar and the cosmic eras represented were common knowledge in Mesoamerica for over a thousand years and not exclusively Aztec. However the Aztecs were the only people to have made a great monument of it. Mesoamericans in general and the Aztecs in particular were obsessed with time, by events repeating themselves in time, and by the immensity of time, despite the fact that they believed that at some point all time comes to an end. The Calendar Stone is not so much an actual calendar, as a monument to time.

## THE OLMEC COLOSSAL HEADS (SAN LORENZO 1)

Twenty Olmec colossal heads have been found so far, and there may be more hidden in the ground. Only in the 1960s were the Olmec monuments dated to a 1000 BC or earlier—until then they were thought to be very late and of little interest to scholars. The most spectacular head is San Lorenzo No. 1, which is nine feet high, weighing sixteen tons. It was found buried in the earth at the site of San Lorenzo in the tropical isthmus area of Mexico. It now appears that the colossal heads are among the earliest art in Mesoamerica carved in a permanent medium. San Lorenzo 1 is so realistic, with pupils in the eyes and slightly parted fleshy lips, that it is generally believed to be the portrait of some important person. We think that this important person was a ruler, but it has even been suggested that he might have been an enemy prisoner. We do not know the original location of the heads at the site, but possibly they were lined up in rows. San Lorenzo was small, perhaps a ceremonial center or small town, not a large city like the Aztec capital.

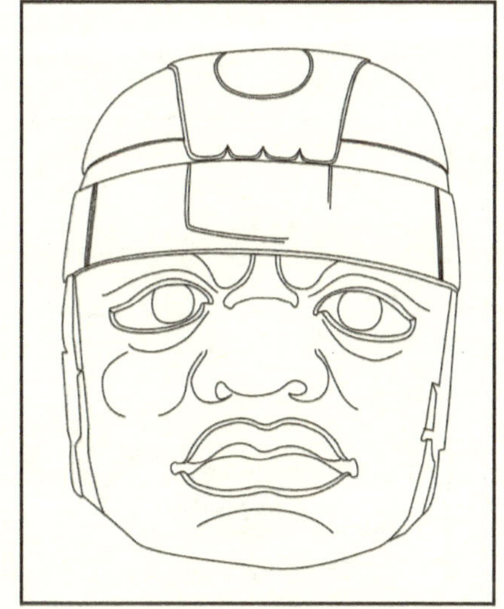

21. Olmec colossal head (San Lorenzo 1).

The astonishing aspect of San Lorenzo 1 is its realism at the very beginning of Mesoamerica's carving tradition. The imitation of nature, or *mimesis* to use Aristotle's term, was the noblest enterprise of the ancient classical artist and has been so in many periods in Western art. In the eighteenth century, Winckelmann demonstrated the gradual steps by which conventionalized Egyptian art turned into realistic Greek art. Not only was Greek art believed to be better, the acquisition of the skills needed were developed gradually over a long period of time. Subsequently, Greek realism was associated with the political concepts of democracy and individualism, characterizing these other admirable traits. Realism has been associated with advanced civilization in the thought of the West.

The majestic head of San Lorenzo 1 challenges some of these ideas. First of all, it suggests that realism need not have had a long period of development, that it is available to the artist when so commissioned and that the more conventionalized works are intentionally so and not due to lack of skill. In fact, not all of Olmec sculpture is equally realistic; there are quite conventionalized works contemporary with the heads. The colossal heads, therefore, challenge one to rethink the whole idea of realism. If realism is not that difficult to achieve, why have not more people at more times desired it? Does it have some undesirable aspects? There are people who have found realism undesirable in that it might "steal the soul" of the person depicted and pose a danger. As we are Westerners imbued with Western values, we can't but be amazed at these early portraits carved in stone with stone tools.

The African features of the face have long been noticed, but they can be an exaggeration of certain Mesoamerican facial types. Though we consider these images "portraits," they may represent idealized rather than individualized representations. As we learn more about the Olmecs, the riddle of the colossal heads may one day be solved.

## THE PYRAMID OF THE SUN AT TEOTIHUACÁN

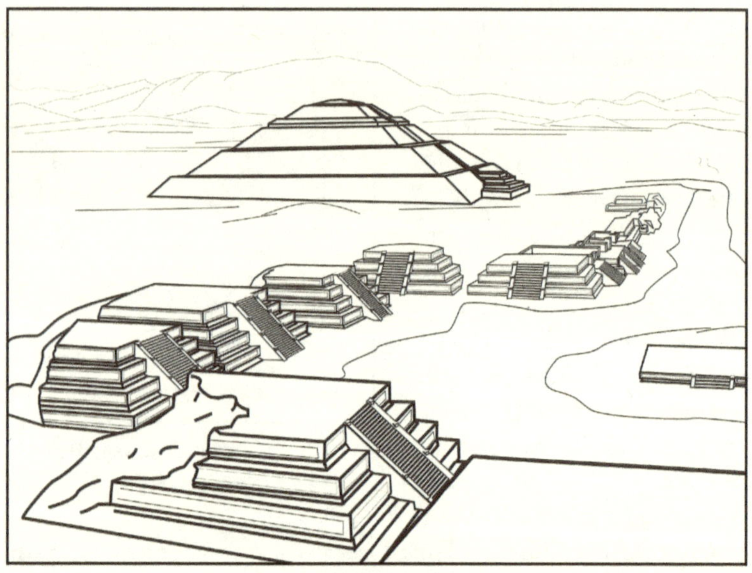

Fig. 22. Teotihuacán Pyramid of the Sun.

The Pyramid of the Sun at Teotihuacán excites admiration because of its huge size—it is always compared to the largest pyramid in Egypt at Giza, which it equals in mass though not quite in height. At 213 feet in height and with a base of 738 square feet, it is a truly impressive architectural monument and proof of the social and labor organization of Teotihuacán about 1 AD. Nor does the pyramid exist by itself; an only somewhat smaller pyramid, the Pyramid of the Moon, is located not far from it at the end of a broad, 131-foot-wide avenue. And an elaborately ornamented pyramid of smaller size is to the south of the Pyramid of the Sun. The ensemble as a whole creates the most gigantic architectural complex ever built in ancient times in the Americas.

The names, Pyramids of the Sun and Moon, were given to these structures by the Spanish, perhaps on the basis of Aztec precedent. The site was too big and too close to Mexico City ever to be "lost," since it remained visible even when overgrown. The Pyramid of the Sun was excavated on the occasion of the inauguration of Porfirio Diaz at the beginning of the twentieth century, and a great deal of surface material was removed, indicating that the structure was originally higher, and its profile is believed to be incorrectly restored. (It was probably 250 feet in height.) The pyramids of Teotihuacán are popularly believed to be Aztec, but they were actually built around the time of Christ, fourteen hundred years before the Aztecs came to power. Since Teotihuacán collapsed in the seventh century, no written sources are available for it.

The "pyramids" of Mexico were really temples. A small building was usually on top of the great stepped platforms. The small rooms served as repositories for images and ritual paraphernalia, and very few people other than rulers and priests ever entered it. The Aztecs sacrificed victims on top of the platforms, and people watched the ceremonies from below.

In the case of the Teotihuacán Pyramid of the Sun, any ritual on top would have looked very small to people below. In the interior mass of pyramids, there were sometimes burials, offerings, and even household refuse. But no royal burial has ever been found at Teotihuacán, raising questions about its political organization.

Prior to the Aztec capital, Teotihuacán was the largest city of its time in Mexico, with a population estimated at two hundred thousand at its height. The apartment compounds in which much of the population lived are visible between and behind the civic structures. However, the language people spoke and the ethnic group they belonged to are still a mystery. The great pyramids were built in the beginning of the city's history, when Teotihuacán was planned. Its astronomical orientation (15.25 degrees east of true north) and great avenue indicate that it was a city planned on a grid. Unlike the Aztec and the Olmec, who put their effort into colossal sculptures, Teotihuacán had the resources to create huge architectural spaces. Curiously, no carved monument shows the rulers of Teotihuacán, suggesting that like the Aztecs the rulers presented the cosmos instead, without their mediation. The cosmos in Teotihuacán's figurative art is mostly that of a benign, verdant nature, rather than the fearsome face of destruction. The pyramids, avenue and courts of Teotihuacán present great spaces for rituals, and since most everyone lived in the city, live rituals rather than representations in stone may have been more immediate.

## THE SARCOPHAGUS OF PACAL AT PALENQUE

For the West, the classic Maya became known as the "Greeks of the New World" because of their elegant, naturalistic art style and their intellectual accomplishments, especially in astronomy. The cultures having fallen by the time of the Spanish conquest, the Maya monuments were discovered mostly in the eighteenth and nineteenth centuries by official and private explorers interested in ruins and ancient peoples. There is no one Maya monument that became the center of interest like the Calendar Stone, since there were a number of Maya regions from Mexico to Honduras, and beautiful works were found in many of them. Perhaps the best-known sites are Palenque and Copán. In 1952 a unique tomb was excavated at Palenque with a very large carved sarcophagus that has now become the most famous Maya image.

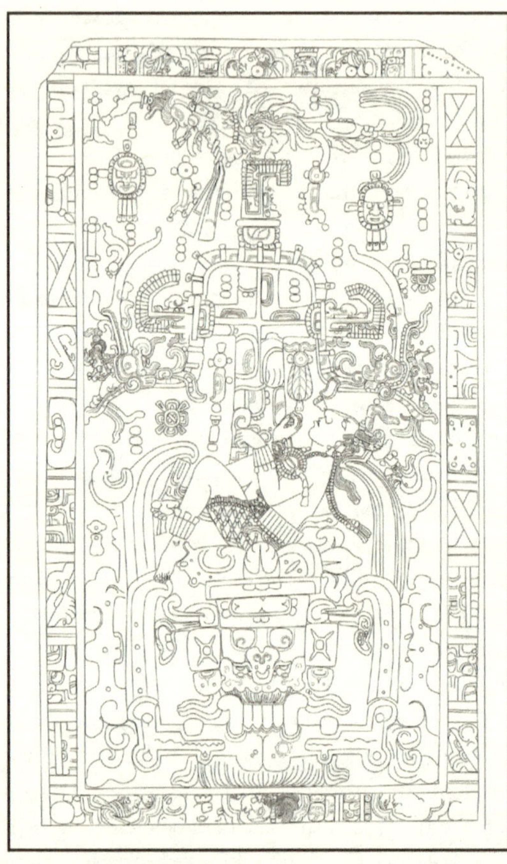

Fig. 23. Sarcophagus of Pacal at Palenque.

The reason the Maya are loved by us is because most of their art depicts idealized human figures now known to be rulers. In their elegant outlines and skimpy attire, they are reminiscent of Greek art. Also, their facial expression is dignified and detached, suggesting the aristocratic values of restraint and self-control we associate with classical art. Recent studies of hieroglyphic writing and vase painting suggest a more Dionysian image of the Maya, with sacrifices, bloodletting, and hallucinatory drugs. However these do not change the appearance of the sculptures whose initial impression has not been affected. Most still consider the Maya the most beautiful ancient American tradition.

On the sarcophagus lid, the elegant, aristocratic ruler is represented as a near naked figure reclining between symbolic imagery above and below him. The complex design is a chart of the cosmos like the Calendar Stone. Above him is a treelike cross representing the upper world and below him is a skull mask, representing the underworld. A double-headed serpent bar, symbolic of rulership, is draped on the "tree," and dynastic deities emerge from its jaws. Epigraphic studies have shown that the ruler's name was Pacal (or Shield) and that he was the first important ruler of the site of Palenque. About 670 AD, he built the Temple of the Inscriptions, in the crypt of which the sarcophagus was placed, untouched until it was excavated in 1952.

Pacal was the major builder of Palenque and probably the creator of its art style. Most of his artistic activities may have been due to the fact that his accession to the dynastic throne was irregular and needed to be propped up by propaganda. All this we know from the recent rich decipherment of Maya glyphs, the most complex writing system in the New World. Maya texts emphasize the ancestry and doings of the rulers, much as Maya art does in images. From texts we know that the artistic spirit behind the greatest art and architecture was often a single ruler with a particular message and resources to make it a reality. This was probably true in other cultures, but either the information is very brief, as in the case of the Aztecs, or we lack the information altogether.

The Maya city-states were much smaller than the empires of the Aztecs or Teotihuacán. Public art focused on the rulers, since the rulers were the centers around which the polities were organized. The largest building at Palenque is the Palace with rooms arranged around courtyards in the very center of the site. Dynastic legitimacy was paramount and Pacal's distinguished ancestors were carved on the sides of the sarcophagus to support his claims. In the importance of forging kin and non-kin alliances, the rulers presented themselves as non-threatening and attractive humans managing the world of the sacred. Portraits of personages are carved in the borders of the sarcophagus with their names indicating the importance of the individual in these relatively small and intimate courts.

## TEMPLES OF TIKAL

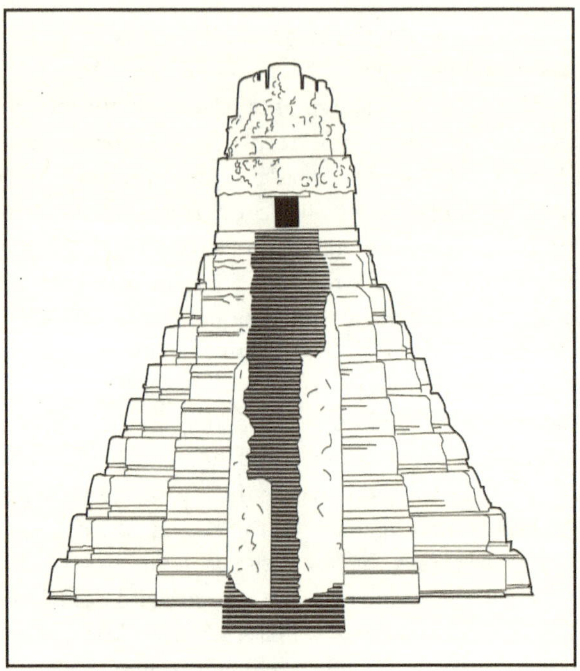

Fig. 24. Tikal Temple I.

No Mesoamerican site is more spectacular to the tourist than the tall pyramids of Tikal in the Guatemalan jungle with spider monkeys playing in the treetops. The five Tikal pyramids are so tall (Temple IV is the tallest at 212 feet), they project over the hundred-foot-high forest. Like all Mesoamerican pyramids, they were built of earth fill, stone retaining walls, and covered with a layer of plaster. The Tikal pyramids are especially elegant with their steep stairways, overlapping apron moldings, and inset corners. Moreover, the buildings on top still exist with the tall crests above them, known as "combs," completing the vertical line. They still exist because the Maya used corbel vaulting to roof their ceremonial buildings. Most Mesoamerican roofs were flat mortar-and-beam constructions. The Maya created vaults by placing stones progressively closer together until they could be spanned by a capstone. This resulted in small, narrow rooms. The roof combs too are lightened by vaulted spaces inside. The soft limestone of the area makes fine stone carving possible, and the moist climate helps the stones in the vaults to bond together.

At Tikal two such pyramids face each other across a plaza (Temple I and Temple II), and the plaza is closed in on the other sides by two complex agglomerations of buildings. There are avenues at Tikal, but they don't obviously lead to these pyramids, giving the assemblage a sense of delightful asymmetry. The grid plan and massiveness of Teotihuacán are often contrasted with the openness and slenderness of Tikal architecture. These two sites, over five hundred miles apart, were the major powers of their time, and judging by Tikal reliefs were in frequent political contact with one another, if not war. The differences in their layout were not just differences in their cultures but differences they chose to emphasize as indicators of their identity.

Temples I and II were built by a ruler designated as A or Ah Cacau (c. 700 AD ), who was buried with a great quantity of jade and other treasures inside Temple I. Temple II, more squat in proportions, may be that of his wife, but this is uncertain. Star Wars filmed Temple IV, a little further out form the center, the largest of the five Tikal pyramids dedicated to A's grandson, ruler C.

Some of the buildings between Temple I and Temple II were either smaller temples crowded on a platform (the North Acropolis) or an enormous palace (the Central Acropolis). Prior to the great ruler A, all the previous rulers were buried in the temples of the North Acropolis. Ruler A, who was a restorer of grandiose power at Tikal, had his pyramids in the open spaces—and later his sons followed suit to even more spectacular places—and was, with the avenues, the grand designer of the city. The palace was built by accretion over centuries and had half a dozen major courts, reception rooms, residential areas, and in some sections five stories with corbelled vaults. Graffiti left by the ancient inhabitants is found in many rooms incised in the plaster.

Tikal sculpture is not considered to be as beautiful as Palenque sculpture. It does not emphasize the graceful human being that we like so much. It focuses more on detail and insignia rather than intimate contact with the viewer. It would appear that the rulers of Tikal were primarily interested in creating an impressive site rather than friendly portraits of themselves. Tikal was larger and more powerful than Palenque and evidently did not need to seduce its allies or supporters by elegance since it awed them by power.

## CHICHÉN ITZÁ

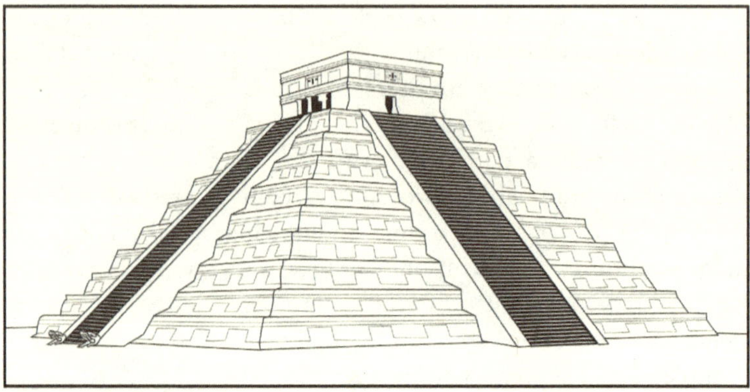

Fig. 25. Chichén Itzá view of the Castillo

Restored largely in the 1930s during work by the Carnegie Institution of Washington, Chichén Itzá has been a magnet for tourism for nearly a century. Its sculptures influenced Modernists such as Henry Moore, who thought preconquest Mexican sculpture was the greatest in the world. He saw Chichén in photographs and books. For the tourists on the ground, one draw has been the cenote, the large sinkhole into which human victims and treasures of gold were thrown. Another is the great ball court, the largest and most decorated in Mesoamerica (497 feet long, 118 feet wide). Rubber which comes from tropical American trees was the material of the ball, and the game was played by teams. Our rubber ball games originate in the Mesoamerican ball game. Not to be touched by hands and feet, in Mesoamerica the game was played with the hip. Putting a shot through a stone hoop high on the wall by a shot from the hip must have been a rare feat. Spectators on the top of the walls watched as the players scored off the walls below. Carved scenes on the benches of the court show ballplayers with one being decapitated, a ritual that may have happened after some special games. The plants growing out of the decapitated heads suggest that the sacrifice was probably meant to bring fertility.

The importance of the ballgame at Chichén Itzá is indicated by the fact that four small temples are attached to the ball court. One of these, the Upper Temple of the Jaguars, had a common Chichén architectural feature, serpents with their heads on the ground supporting a lintel. These serpent columns are dynamic, organic forms in the midst of rectilinear architecture, an innovation at Chichén Itzá.

The special feature of Chichén Itzá is the heterogeneity of its architectural styles, raising so-far unanswered questions about its political structure and history. Recent studies suggest a councilor government. Some buildings such as the ball court are carved with relatively simple relief figures in many scenes. Other parts of the site, such as the Monjas, are in the local Puuc Maya style of stone mosaic ornamentation and have no relief figures. Some buildings have Classic Maya inscriptions. Some buildings such as the Temple of the Warriors have both relief figures and mosaic wall panels, suggesting that these are more or less contemporary or at least mixable. At Chichén Itzá one faces a site that was created possibly by different ethnic groups and/or lineages living together and creating in different and merging styles. The fascination to the visitor is seeing all these different styles in one site.

Chichén Itzá was not just eclectic, it was also innovative, especially in buildings with astronomical features. The central pyramid, known as the Castillo, is the largest at the site, with 365 steps on its four stairways and 52 panels on its sides. It is oriented in such a way that during the equinoxes sunlight casts a shadow of the rectangular panels of its stages revealing a "serpent of light" alongside the stairway. The serpent of light seems to descend from the serpent columns of the building on top to a serpent head at its base, which seems to point in the direction of the cenote. Buildings demonstrating astronomical phenomena are known at other Mesoamerican sites, but none as dramatic as the Castillo. Most interestingly, Chichén also has an actual observatory.

The Chichén Itzá observatory, the Caracol, is unique in Mesoamerica. It is a round building with a handsome five-part Puuc Maya-style molding where the roof meets the walls, as well as curving corbel vaults. Reliefs indicate that it is an eclectic building. Small windows were placed so that the observance of the synodic periods of the planet Venus were visible. Observations included the solstices and equinoxes, as well as stars like the Pleiades.

It has been noted since the nineteenth century that there are parallels in the architecture of Chichén Itzá and Tula in central Mexico. This has usually been explained by the legend of Quetzalcoatl who was a Toltec king exiled from Tula, who is supposed to have left and conquered Maya Chichén. According to this view, the Toltecs of Tula introduced their style into the preexisting Maya Puuc style. According to this version, Chichén dates mostly after 1000 AD, when the Toltecs were in power at Tula.

According to recent theory, all the people of Chichén Itzá were Maya of different localities, and the buildings were more or less contemporary, dating to 900 AD or even earlier, coeval with Tikal or Palenque. Some suggest that because it was so cosmopolitan and innovative, Chichén Itzá was more likely the influence on the provincial site of Tula and not the other way around. Chichén Itzá has lacked large-scale excavation, and many of the interpretations about it are still very speculative. The heterogeneity of Chichén Itzá in contrast to the homogeneity of Teotihuacán or Tikal makes it feel like a modern city.

## THE CODEX BORGIA

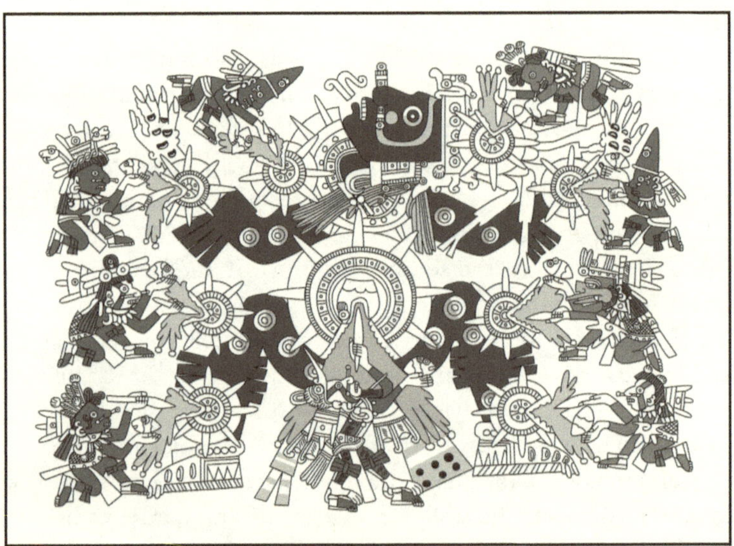

Fig. 26. Codex Borgia, Vatican Library.

Only fourteen preconquest books survive from Mesoamerica, because of the tropical climate and the Spanish book-burning. Of these the largest and most impressively painted is in the Vatican library. It shows signs of burning, either from having been taken away from children who were playing with it as a toy until c. 1800 or from earlier missionary book-burning. The book was ultimately in the collection of Cardinal Stefano Borgia, whose name it bears. It was most likely sent to Europe from Mexico as an example of New World things in the sixteenth century.

Its preconquest origin is unknown, but its style is close to the works in the area of the city of Cholula in the state of Puebla and in the Mixteca region of western Oaxaca. It is not Aztec, though there are similarities with Aztec style. It may date to the fifteenth century.

Screen-fold books of native paper or deer hide such as the Codex Borgia may go back in Mesoamerica to AD 1 or even earlier and are frequently depicted on Maya vases. They combine figures and scenes with glyphs.

There exist also three Maya books which have longer texts than the Codex Borgia. The Mixteca-Puebla books tell their stories more with images. The Borgia Codex is religious and was probably the property of a diviner or priest who calibrated the day signs and deities with the numbers in foretelling lucky and unlucky days and personal fortunes. Much of the manuscript deals with the day signs of the calendar and their deity patrons in various arrangements. These indicate the complexity of the calendar and of esoteric knowledge that the Spanish texts of the sixteenth century do not explain. Various figures, such as the deity Tezcatlipoca, have day signs associated with various parts of their bodies, suggesting ways in which the day signs were related to many aspects of things and beings. The more complex aspects of divination and of the gods have, unfortunately, not come down to us, but they are there in the Codex Borgia to be deciphered still.

Even more mysterious than the day signs are the so-called "underworld journey" pages, which depict little figures in a realm of death and sacrifice that could illustrate several themes, according to recent scholars, such a rituals, creation myths, and/or initiation rites for rulers. According to some accounts, many rulers went to the city of Cholula to be confirmed in their rule by the powerful cult of Quetzalcoatl and his priests. This section of the codex is still a challenge for interpretation.

Mesoamerican books included dynastic histories, divinatory calendars, maps, tribute accounts, and probably other subjects we are unaware of. They could have used native paper or deer hide for more incidental writing purposes that are now lost, such as letters. The beauty of the Codex Borgia lies in its controlled line that silhouettes the figures and the bright colors that fill the resulting areas.

## THE ANDES

Mesoamerican art is familiar to the West in its figuration, realism, narrative, and monumental stone carving. Andean art is stranger in its obsession with yarn and seems not based primarily on images but resides in structures and techniques. Andeans worked with and thought with fibers—the earliest surviving art is that of cotton textiles; even the Inca royal headdress was a red wool fringe and not a gold crown. Rivers were crossed by suspension bridges made from ropes.

The Central Andean area comprises mostly modern Peru and Bolivia, although in the late period it included Ecuador, Northwest Argentina, and Northern Chile as well. Civilization in the Andes began in the preceramic period (4000–1000 BC), prior to pottery and most agriculture, because the cold Humboldt Current off the coast teams with marine life that made permanent settlement possible. These fishing cultures erected hundreds of monumental architectural sites, of which Aspero is one of the most outstanding. The earliest textiles go back to the preceramic period, when cotton and gourds were grown. The first figurative art style of the Andes is Chavín, named after the site of Chavín de Huántar, a style that is found in various forms throughout the Andes, especially in the Early Horizon period, 1000–200 BC.

The best known cultures of the Andes are the Moche of the north coast and Paracas and Nazca on the south coast, known mainly for their ceramics and textiles, respectively. Metalwork was very sophisticated among the Moche. While the representations of the Moche are more realistic and those of Paracas and Nazca are more fantastic, both show the natural and supernatural world in immense detail. Politically, the area was divided into small warring kingdoms, and this so-called Early Intermediate period (200 BC–600 AD) was a time of regional isolation. One of the first possible empires in the area, Tiahuanaco in Bolivia, had its roots in this period, but its florescence was in the Middle Horizon (600–1000 AD). Tiahuanaco is known for its exceptional stone masonry and stone carving of figures.

Huari in Peru shared many stylistic and religious ideas with Tiahuanaco and was the center of an empire spreading to the north. Andean empires all originated in the highlands. In the Late Intermediate period (1000–1450 AD), the major power was the Chimú kingdom on the north coast, known for its adobe architecture, textiles and metalwork. A large quantity of gold and silver objects have come from the Chimú and further north the Sicán cultures, most of which have been looted as far back as the seventeenth century, not just the present. Gold-working in the Andes goes back to 2000 BC.

The Inca reigned in Peru for about as long as the Aztecs in Mexico (Late Horizon, 1450–1531 AD). They conquered the area from their capital city, Cuzco. Unlike the Aztec empire, which was based on tribute, the Inca empire was territorially controlled over a three-thousand-mile distance, from Ecuador to Chile. Monumental architecture and an elaborate road system were the Inca's major achievements. The Inca were not particularly interested in figurative representation. All Andean cultures were more interested in the ideas behind their representations than in the imitation of reality. On some occasions, their works were actually invisible to the eye and evident only to the mind.

## THE KHIPU (QUIPU)

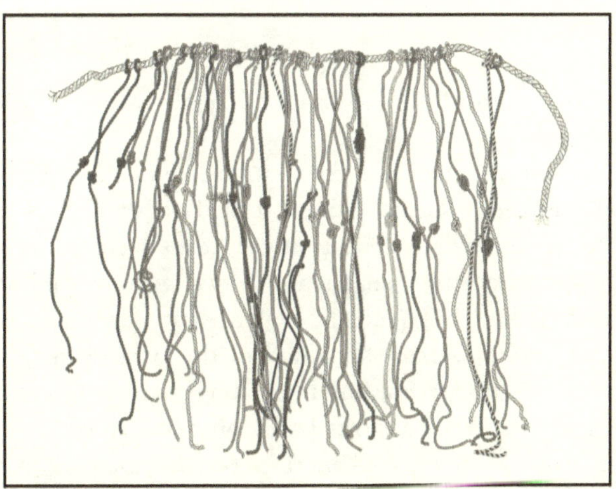

Fig. 27. The Inca khipu.

The Andean recording device was not a book with writing but knotted cords tied together. In the sixteenth century they were thought to be a simple mnemonic device, like a rosary, but recently they have been shown to be quite sophisticated. Meaning has now been found in the color of the strings, the direction of spinning, the way the knots were made, and other structural features. Most of these features come in twos, so that the khipu maker had to choose one of two alternatives for a particular bit of information. The system, therefore, was based on a binary principle. As has long been known, khipu were primarily numerical accounts based on the decimal counting of things like census figures or storehouse contents, although calendrical information and histories are also known to be recorded. It is clear in the case of the khipu that information was not stored in images, or glyphs derived from images, but in conceptual relationships based on a binary system. Khipus functioned somewhat like a computer, and only in our computer age has the complexity of the khipu been deciphered.

The khipu fit well with the things recorded: Andean polities kept track of births, deaths, and populations, as well as goods collected and redistributed by the states. Instead of a market system as in Mesoamerica, Andean trade was based mostly on exchange among real or fictive kin. Of the six hundred or so existing khipus, most are Inca or late in date, although simpler earlier versions probably existed in the Middle Horizon period.

## MOCHE PORTRAIT HEADS

Most Andean representation is conventionalized or abstract except for some Moche images, especially the so-called portrait heads in ceramic. As early as the nineteenth century these heads were admired because of their realistic depiction suggesting actual persons, old and young, frowning and smiling, but generally looking quite dignified. Nearly eight hundred such head vessels are known, depicting possibly fifty individuals. Many of these vessels are fine and interesting, and my choice of the one at the Art Institute of Chicago is based on personal preference. There is no particular one that seems more important than the others, since they generally come from illegal excavations without provenience. Like Roman Republican portraits, the heads appear to represent statesmen with elite headgear, penetrating eyes, aquiline noses, and narrow lips. It is quite obvious that Andean artists were perfectly capable of modeling realistic images when commissioned to do so. The mystery for the Westerner is that most of the time they chose not to. Even the heads, which seem to be such an accomplishment in our eyes, were made for a short time in a small area of the Moche zone, and nothing like it was ever made again. Apparently Andeans didn't see this as an "artistic" advance.

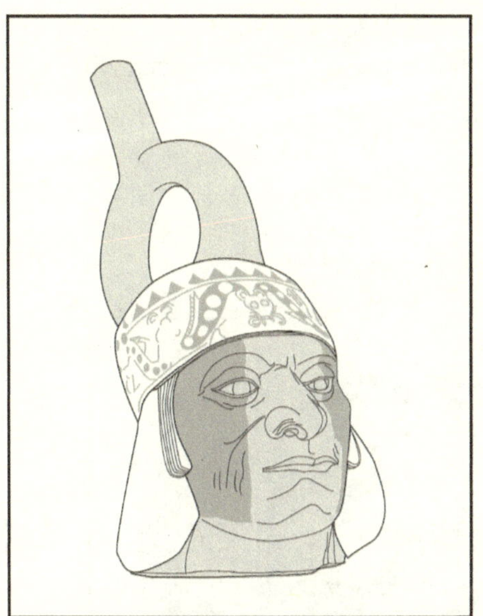

Fig. 28. Moche portrait head vessel, Art Institute of Chicago.

The Moche portrait heads were made mostly in Phase 4, c. 400 to 500 AD, in five river valleys in the southern Moche area. The rest of the Moche area had a more conventionalized and less personal style. For art historical theory this raises the question of what the role of realism is in a non-Western context. Since Moche culture is known only archaeologically, any answers are hypothetical and tentative. Our interpretation has generally been that these heads are "rulers" or otherwise important men. As they were made in molds and there are duplications, we don't know who owned them and why. They are usually found in burials along with other vessels. Though we emphasize the portraits, they are actually vessels with handles and spouts, like all other Moche containers. Most Andean ceramics were vessels with a partially utilitarian purpose. Such vessels probably contained a liquid, water or maize beer, for the dead in the afterworld.

According to recent analysis, some of the heads represent individuals who had been captured and killed. This raises some interesting questions about realism—we assume that realism is a mark of honor, but the Moche may have seen it as a mark of humiliation. Given the fact that the heads were made in a short time and small area, there may have been a particular vogue to commemorate certain persons by the resemblance of their actual physiognomy, either because they were greatly admired or greatly despised. In either case, realism was something very powerful and generally shunned for most other representations.

Another issue raised by the Moche portrait heads is the acquisition of skills needed for realistic representation. The Moche went from stylized Phase 3 heads to naturalistic Phase 4 ones in a short time, quite easily, suggesting that there were no great technical difficulties involved in naturalistic representation. This indicates that the issues are ideological and political rather than technical. The Moche political situation is not well enough known at present, but warring polities sharing the same culture are quite likely.

## THE PARACAS TEXTILE

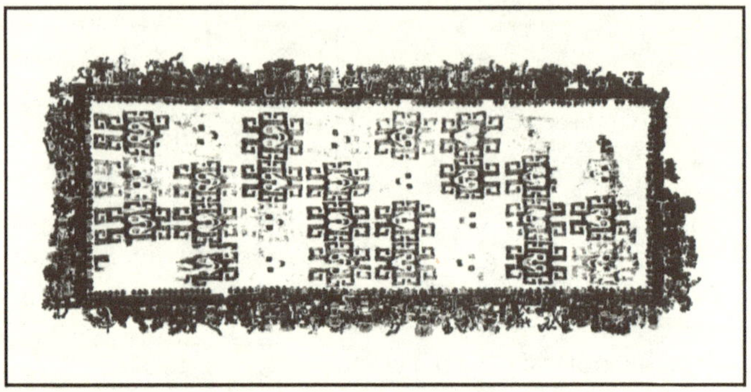

Fig. 29. Paracas Textile, the Brooklyn Museum.

Andean weavers invented every known technique of preindustrial weaving and a few more of their own. In the burials of the desert coast, many textiles have survived in remarkable preservation, of which the most famous is the Paracas textile, now in the Brooklyn Museum. This textile was found in 1911 and in the '20s and '30s was exhibited in Paris and New York as something rare and curious. Its finding led in 1925 to the excavation of the tombs of the Paracas peninsula on the southern coast of Peru, in which over four hundred mummy bundles were found wrapped in hundreds of textiles. Despite such numerous finds, the Paracas textile in the Brooklyn Museum remains unique and special, in some ways the most complex textile known to us from Peru. It probably dates 1 to 400 AD.

Most Andean textiles are garments such as mantles, loincloths, tunics, and turbans. The Brooklyn textile is not a garment but a ceremonial cloth. The center field consists of warp-wrapped mask faces (thirty-two of the thirty-four remain), but the real interest in the cloth is the fringe of about ninety little figures in the border. Each of these figures is half woven into the border and half projecting three-dimensionally. There are sixty distinct personages, some repeated, male and female, combined

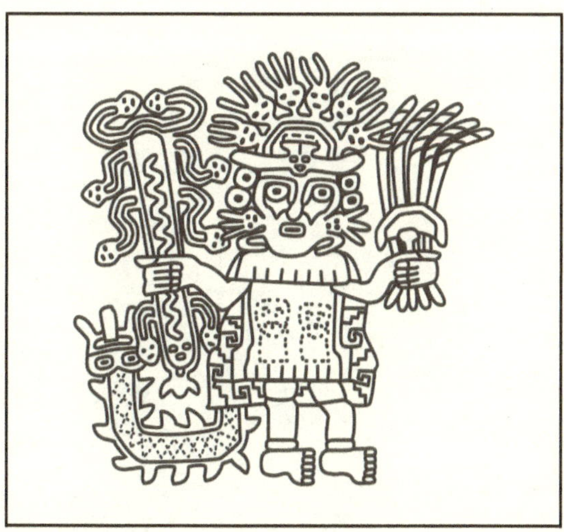

Fig. 30. Paracas Textile, personage from the fringe detail.

with animal and plant forms. There are not central figures, so the images seem to be multiple and equally important spirit beings in profusion. The colors are remarkably bright testifying to the art of dying camelid wool in the Andes.

The technique of making the three-dimensional figures is described as "needle-knitting." The little figures are combinations of humans, plants, and animals. In fact, however, they are literally growing in and out of each other in curving shapes. In one figure, a tree grows through the body of a feline, and in another tropical plants like manioc grow from the body of a llama. The basic theme seems to be the interconnectedness of nature. Images of gold ornaments of status are intertwined between the living forms, referring clearly to human society. While we do not know who these spirits were exactly, they indicate both a rich supernatural world and a sophisticated human world that invented them.

The Paracas textile is sometimes considered to be a codex in cloth. Much as Mesoamericans painted their views of the supernatural in books, Andeans wove them into cloth; it just took us longer to recognize them as intellectual constructs because of their unexpected format.

## THE NAZCA LINES

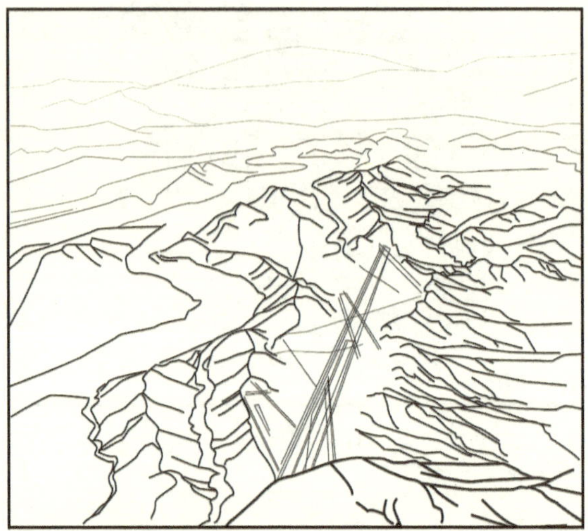

Fig. 31. Lines in the Nazca Plateau

The Nazca lines are probably the best known works of ancient Peru. Their attraction lies in their mystery—how and why did Andeans make straight lines and figures on a desert plateau when they could not even see them? It was probably conceptual art and earth art of the 1970s that led to their popularization, but in fact earth art was inspired by works like the Nazca lines, making the relationship circular. The Nazca lines were discovered through aviation, raising the question of how the Natives could have created them without seeing them. Like Tikal, the lines have been candidates for extraterrestrial agency.

The lines are on a dry plateau and were made by removing the dark oxidized surface stones to the edges of the lines, revealing a lighter "path" in between. Since broken pottery found on the plateau dates to the Nazca period, they are believed to have been made from 1 AD to 600 AD. Some lines are as long as a mile and perfectly straight. Many radiate from a central hub like the spokes of a wheel. Lines go over each other and over the figurative forms. The figurative forms of plants and animals were made by a continuous line, suggesting that ropes may have been used to lay out the designs. The purpose of the lines is still a mystery. Generally, they are not astronomical. It has recently been suggested that they indicated water sources. Perhaps they were ritual paths for processions in certain lineages. As mental images invisible from the ground, they are characteristic of the Andean view of the world, and it is not surprising that we see them as one of the great wonders of the ancient world.

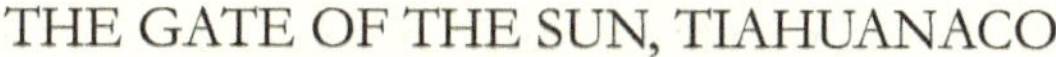

## THE GATE OF THE SUN, TIAHUANACO

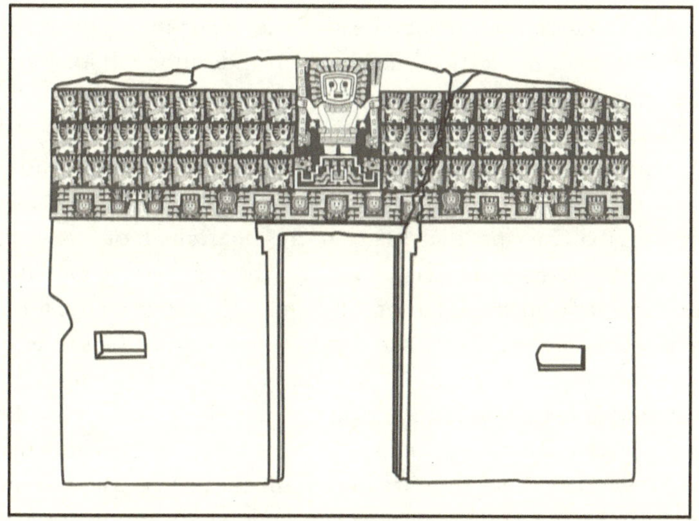

32. Tiahuanaco Gate of the Sun

The oldest Andean work to have been admired by Westerners is the so called Gate of the Sun at Tiahuanaco that was already known to the conquerors and chroniclers in the sixteenth century and was a goal of traveler-explorers in the eighteenth. All of them were amazed by the large size (10 feet high) and weight of this monolithic stone. The central face with rays suggested the "sun" appellation to the Spanish and perhaps to the Inca as well. Carved between 500 and 1000 AD, the work is pre-Inca, and its site, a temple city, was in ruins by the time the Inca came to power. The Inca were so impressed by the ruins of Tiahuanaco that they wanted similar fine stonework in their capital city of Cuzco. Tiahuanaco was an empire with its center near Lake Titicaca in Bolivia, extending primarily to the south.

The Gate of the Sun is a marvel of precise cutting in stone, which is a hard andesite. The upper or lintel half is carved with a three-dimensional central figure surrounded by rows of winged profile figures in relief. The design is angular and geometric with sharply incised lines. The frontal central figure with the rays around his head appears to be a deity, while the bird- and human-headed human figures seem to be attendants. The precision and symmetrical layout of the design makes it look very imposing. The monument seems to be about power—human power and supernatural power. In the lowest register, there are two tiny human figures indicating hierarchy by scale in which the human counts for little. The human figures hold trophy heads. The collecting of trophy heads was a widespread Andean custom and an indication of long-standing warring and hostility among neighboring groups. Trophy heads were believed to increase human and natural fertility.

That the Gate of the Sun became the favorite work of Andean art among Westerners is due to the fact of its large size and in some ways comprehensible carving that made it the equivalent of the Calendar Stone of the Aztecs. In fact, various scholars have counted heads and other details on the Gate of the Sun, suggesting that it too was a calendar. (The Paracas textile has also been considered by some to have been a calendar.) It is not impossible that calendrical notations were in carvings and in textiles as in the khipu, but it is also possible that the very organized, chart-like and structured aspects of Andean works make us think of calendars. Calendars are important for us because they indicate the supposed intellectual level of a civilization. Andean images may be more metaphoric views of the organization of the cosmos than specific calendars but may be intellectual in their ways just the same.

## SICÁN GOLD MASK

Peru is associated with gold, and the most spectacular pieces come from the Sicán culture. Almost all Inca gold was melted down by the Spanish during the conquest. The Inca ruler Atahuallpa was taken prisoner and promised a ransom if he filled a room with gold and two with silver. The rooms were filled, but of course Atahuallpa was executed in order to remove the Inca leadership. The gold and silver were melted down. This oversized Sicán mask is from an earlier archaeological context. A great deal of gold and silver in Peru is unfortunately mostly looted. Gold

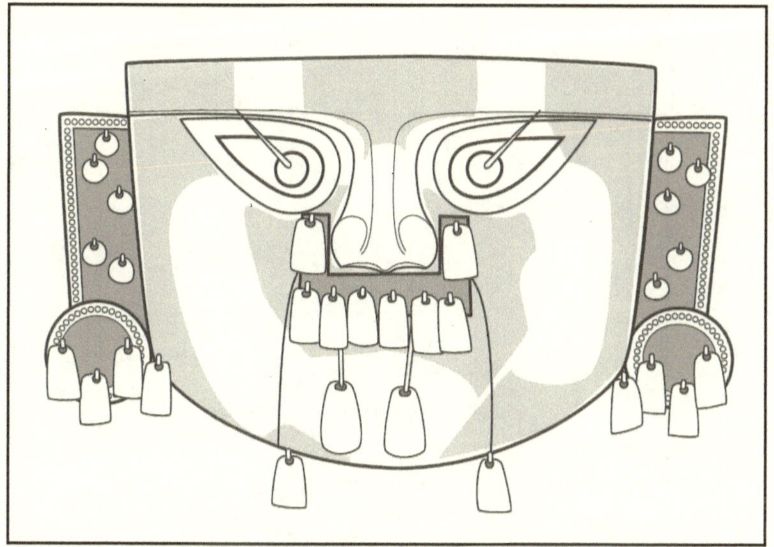

Fig. 33. Gold mask, Sicán culture.

masks such as this are especially significant for having red paint covering the gold surface, a practice strange from the point of view of the West, where we want to see the gold as material. In the Andes however, things did not have to be seen to be appreciated. So long as it was known that the gold was there, its surface could be something else. Andean concern is more with the inner essence of things than with their visible appearance.

The Sicán culture, 1000 to 1200 AD, was located on the far north coast of Peru. It is best known for its lavish burials with hundreds of gold objects, such as cups, knives, and masks. Most of these have been obtained by looters and therefore little information is available on the context and meaning of the masks. Made by hammering, the masks have a slightly textured surface characteristic of Andean metalwork.

## MACHU PICCHU

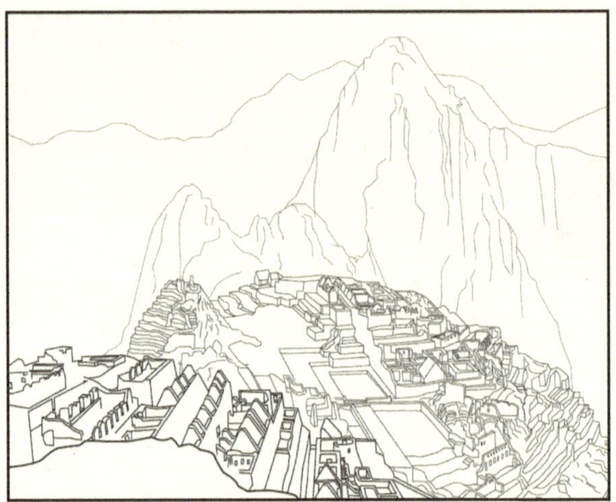

Fig. 34. View of Machu Picchu.

In 1911 Hiram Bingham, a Yale University professor, was exploring the Andean mountains and "found" Machu Picchu with the help of Native guides. This means primarily that he publicized the existence of ruins previously known to locals and a few others. The site of Machu Picchu was a spectacular discovery, because it seemed to have played no role in the Spanish conquest, was not mentioned in the sixteenth-century chronicles, and was undamaged. One could put new thatched roofs on the buildings and move back in. Moreover the site is in a magnificent location, in a U-shaped bend of the Urubamba River, surrounded by mountains on a saddle between two peaks. It was already a romantic tourist spot in the 1930s. The stonework is fine Inca masonry consisting of well-fitting stones with gentle, pillowy outer curvatures. Here and there the natural rock of the terrain has been worked into buildings, suggesting sacred shrines or rocks, such as the tower with its cave and rock.

Machu Picchu is not mentioned in any sixteenth-century literature directly, and archaeological excavations have revealed relatively little. Most recent interpretations suggest that it was an estate of the first powerful king, Pachacuti. As a site apparently inhabited only occasionally, no more than a few thousand people were ever there, and the limited water source was adequate for them.

Pachacuti was the military leader who created the Inca state and began some of the major conquests. He is believed to have devised the Inca architectural style with its emphasis on beautiful views, incorporation of natural rocks, and precise but slightly irregular masonry. Some of his ideas may have come from the ruins of Tiahuanaco. But the Inca did not personify the forces of nature in anthropomorphic deities; they used nature as it was. Inca power, therefore, seemed to spring literally out of the earth and blend seamlessly into masonry.

The Inca and many other Andeans believed that the task of good government was the creation of order and protection of the populace. The Inca modified the kinship-based system of earlier cultures to create a vast area of "reciprocal" relations, from Chile to Ecuador. According to sixteenth-century commentators, there was no poverty in the empire, but everyone's life was strictly regulated. On top of the hierarchy was the Inca ruler with vast personal possessions and estates. Most of the Inca architecture that survives is from Pachacuti's time and expresses his projection of Inca power and values. Unlike the earlier Moche, Paracas, and Tiahuanaco cultures, the sacred was not represented by human figures or animals but by nature in its most basic inorganic forms. Such an ecological art was already present in some earlier arts but greatly expanded by the Inca.

# EPILOGUE

The people, cultures, and arts of the New World have been a vast Rorschach test in which people of the Old World have sought to see their image, their dreams, or their nightmares. The people in art and reality are enough like the rest of us that they can be easily adapted to any enterprise. That many of us are involved in this enterprise suggests that we are still trying to come to terms with the anomaly of New World cultures that we do not understand and can't calibrate with the Old World. Seen as primitives lacking the wheel or extraterrestrials with superior technology, we try to find a mental space for them. The inhabitants of the New World and the fantastic monuments their ancestors left behind are the only "others" we have on this planet to compare to ourselves and thus very precious. Is it any wonder that from time to time we think that in some way they were really us all along?

For a few years there was nothing new in the popular theories about the origins of American Indian cultures, perhaps because no new evidence had come to light that could be interpreted in imaginative new ways. That changed with the 1976 *Viking 1* discovery of a gigantic "face" on Mars. (Best photographs of the Cydonia area of Mars were not made public until 1998.) This face and the associated "figures" have given rise to a small industry of enthusiasts trying to interpret them, mostly from parallels in Mesoamerican, mostly Mayan representations. While NASA insists that these faces are purely accidental photos of rock formations and interpreting them as faces is like seeing figures in clouds, many believe them to be artificial mounds, built by intelligent beings, intended to communicate perhaps with the earth. The faces are in a sector of Mars called Cydonia.

The faces are described as huge "geoglyphs" like the Andean lines and figures on the plateau of the Nazca area. They are mostly in profile, and their full "faces" are discovered by mirroring them—that is by flipping the photographs to the other side. Authors George Haas and William Saunders in their book, *The Cynodia Codex: Reflections from Mars* (2005), analyze the images on the basis of ancient but mostly pre-Columbian parallels. For example, they see the original face as a split representation, one half-human, the other half-feline, similar to an early Mesoamerican clay mask, as well as similarities with the Egyptian lion, which brings the Africans back into Mesoamerica.

In a complicated fable derived from Sumerian mythology, they claim that many centuries before man, c. 500,000 BC, Martian gods came to earth, busy with their own agendas and conflicts, primarily to mine gold. They created humans out of their own DNA and out of the primitive earthlings they encountered (homo erectus). They wanted the people to work for them in the gold mines. This is how the human race was formed. Thus we are all genetically derived from Mars. Quetzalcoatl, the youngest son of a Martian/Sumerian god, known there as Ningishzidda, spread the knowledge of arts, crafts, agriculture, and science in the New World.

While they are not entirely clear on the purpose of the faces on Mars, they suggest that they were built to commemorate the Martians' arrival on earth. The fact that the Martian images can be deciphered through Mesoamerican imagery means that Martians and humans at one time shared the same symbolic language.

This is an ingenious account that brings the popular theories up to date: the real exploration of space with specific monuments and the genetic advances of DNA are included in the story. At the same time, all this Martian account is decoded in terms of the ancient cultures of Mesoamerica and Mesopotamia. The earth is still populated by gods initially, and there is a role for mythic personages like Quetzalcoatl.

Perhaps the most interesting and up-to-date aspect of *The Cydonia Codex*, is its global point of view. Although Mesoamerican imagery had a privileged place in the decipherment process, the ancient peoples are not divided into races or cultures. The Martians do not originate Native Americans in particular. They create the whole human race as a unity. The issues they raise are not between ethnic groups on earth, but between humanity and the cosmos, which might have other beings like us. In the current popular theories, the origin of humankind is as much of a mystery as the origin of the American Indian once was.

# Bibliography


I. American Indians

"Paleoamerican Origins." 2010 In *The Encyclopedia Smithsonian.* Retrieved November 22, 2010, from http://www.si.edu/encyclopedia_si/nmnh/origin.htm.

Sutherton, Simon G. 2004 *Losing a Lost Tribe: Native Americans, DNA, and the Mormon Church.* Salt Lake City: Signature Books.

II. Princess Watahwaso's Teepee

Haviland, William A. 2009 *At the Place of the Lobsters and Crabs: Indian People and Deer Isle, Maine, 1605–2005.* Solon, Maine: Polar Bear & Company.

Wauchope, Robert. 1962 *Lost Tribes and Sunken Continents: Myth and Method in the Study of American Indians.* Chicago: University of Chicago Press.

III. Aliens

Crick, Sir Francis. 1981 *Life Itself: Its Origin and Nature.* New York: Simon and Schuster.

"Erich von Däniken." 2010 In *Wikipedia, The Free Encyclopedia.* Retrieved November 22, 2010, from http://en.wikipedia.org/w/index.php?title=Erich_von_D%C3%A4niken&oldid=397428341.

Jung, Carl G. 1979 *Flying Saucers: A Modern Myth of Things Seen in the Skies.* Princeton: The Princeton University Press Bollingen Series.

McMullen, David. 1997 *Mystery in Peru: The Lines of Nazca.* Great Unsolved Mysteries Series. Raintree Steck-Vaughn Publishers.

Sagan, Carl, L. S. Sagan, and Frank Drake. 1972 "A Message from Earth," in *Science* 175: 4024 (February): pp. 881–884.

Vincenz, Kirsten. 2001 "The Nazca Lines in the Age of Space Travel: Ancient Astronauts and Other Myths," M.A. paper, Columbia University Department of Art History and Archaeology.

Von Däniken, Erich. 1967 *Chariots of the Gods.* New York: G. P. Putnam's Sons.

———. 1973 *The Gold of the Gods.* New York: Bantam Books.

IV. The Lost Tribes of Israel

"2012 Phenomenon." 2010 In *Wikipedia, The Free Encyclopedia.* Retrieved November 22, 2010, from http://en.wikipedia.org/w/index.php?title=2012_phenomenon&oldid=397689281.

Durán, Diego. 1994 *The History of the Indies of New Spain*, trans. Doris Heyden.

Norman: University of Oklahoma Press.

Lafaye, Jacques. 1976 *Quetzalcoatl and Guadalupe: The formation of Mexican national consciousness, 1531–1813*, trans. Benjamin Keen. Chicago: University of Chicago Press.

Las Casas, Bartolomé. 1992 *A Short Account of the Destruction of the Indies*, ed. and trans. Nigel Griffin. London; New York: Penguin Books.

Smith, Joseph, Jr. 1830 *The Book of Mormon*. Salt Lake City: Church of Jesus Christ of Latter-day Saints, [1977].

Warren, Bruce W., and Thomas Stuart Ferguson. 1987 *The Messiah in Ancient America*. Provo, UT: Book of Mormon Research Foundation.

V. Sunken Continents

Churchward, Col. James. 1926 *The Lost Continent of Mu*. Albuquerque, N.M.: Brotherhood of Life, [1987].

———. 1933 *The Sacred Symbols of the Mu*. New York: Paperback Library, Inc. [1968].

"James Churchward." 2010 In *Wikipedia, The Free Encyclopedia*. Retrieved November 22, 2010, from http://en.wikipedia.org/w/index.php?title=James_Churchward&oldid=396853667.

Donnelly, Ignatius. 1882 *Atlantis: The Antediluvian World*. New York: Dover Publications [1976].

Plato. 1945 *The Timæus and Critias, or Atlanticus*, trans. Thomas Taylor. New York: Pantheon Books.

Sclater, Philip. 1864 "The Mammals of Madagascar," in *Quarterly Journal of Science*, vol. 1.

VI. Racial Migrations

Gladwin, Harold S. 1947 *Men Out of Asia*. Columbus, Ohio: McGraw Hill.

Van Sertima, Ivan, ed. 1987 *African Presence in Early America*. New Brunswick, N.J.: Journal of African Civilizations.

———, ed. 1976 *They Came Before Columbus: The African Presence in Ancient America*, New York: Random House, Inc.

Viollet-le-Duc, Eugène-Emmanuel. 1863 *Cités et ruines américaines: Mitla, Palenqué, Izamal, Chichén Itzá, Uxmal*. Paris: Gide et Morel.

Von Wuthenau, Alexander. 1970 *The Art of Terracotta Pottery in Pre-Columbian Central and South America*. Art of the World: The Historical, Sociological, and Religious Backgrounds Series. New York: Crown Publishers.

Whipps, Heather. 2007 "Chicken Bones Suggest Polynesians Found Americas before Columbus," in *LiveScience* (04 June 2007). Retrieved November 22, 2010, from http://www.livescience.com/history/070604_polynesian_chicken.html.

VII. Seagoing Craft

Heyerdahl, Thor. 1950 *Kon-Tiki: Across the Pacific in a Raft.* Chicago: Rand McNally and Co.

———. 1971 *Ra Expeditions*. Sydney: Allen & Unwin Australia.

———. 1974 *Fatu-Hiva: Back to Nature.* Buccaneer Books.

"Junk (ship)." 2010 In *Wikipedia, The Free Encyclopedia.* Retrieved November 22, 2010, from http://en.wikipedia.org/w/index.php?title=Junk_(ship)&oldid=397233582.

Menzies, Gavin. 2002 *1421: The Year China Discovered America.* London and New York: HarperCollins Publishers Inc.

"Outrigger canoe." 2010 In *Wikipedia, The Free Encyclopedia.* Retrieved November 22, 2010, from http://en.wikipedia.org/w/index.php?title=Outrigger_canoe&oldid=397479889.

"Thor Heyerdahl." 2010 In *Wikipedia, The Free Encyclopedia.* Retrieved November 22, 2010, from http://en.wikipedia.org/w/index.php?title=Thor_Heyerdahl&oldid=397491364.

"Viking." 2010 In *Wikipedia, The Free Encyclopedia.* Retrieved November 22, 2010, from http://en.wikipedia.org/w/index.php?title=Viking&olid=396991219.

VIII. The Asiatic Tiger

Ekholm, Gordon, and Robert Heine-Geldern. 1951 "Significant Parallels in the Symbolic Arts of Southern Asia and Middle America," in *The Civilizations of Ancient America, Selected Papers of the 29th International Congress of Americanists*, ed. Sol Tax. Chicago: University of Chicago Press, pp. 299–309.

Evans, Clifford, B. J. Meggers, and E. Estrada. 1959 *Cultura Valdivia.* Publicaciones del Museo Victor Emilio Estrada, no. 6. Guayaquil.

Fraser, Douglas, ed. 1968 *Early Chinese Art and the Pacific Basin: A Photographic Exhibition.* New York: Intercultural Arts Press.

Heine-Geldern, Robert. 1958 "Representations of the Asiatic Tiger in the Art of the Chavín Culture: a proof of early contacts between China and Peru," in *XXXIII Congreso Internacional de Americanistas.* San Jose, Costa Rica, pp. 20–27.

———. 1966 "The Problem of Trans-Pacific Influences in Mesoamerica," in *Handbook of Middle American Indians*, vol. 4, ed. Robert Wauchope. Austin: University of Texas Press, pp. 277–295.

Kelley, David H. 2005 Exploring Ancient Skies: An Encyclopedic Survey of Archaeoastronomy. Berlin: Springer Verlag.

Riley, Carroll R., J. Charles Kelley, Campbell W. Pennington, and Robert L. Rands, eds. 1971 *Man across the Sea: Problems of Pre-Columbian Contacts.* Austin: University of Texas Press.

IX. Great Fakes

Pasztory, Esther. 1983 *Aztec Art.* New York: H. N. Abrams.

———. 2002 "Truth in Forgery," in *RES: Anthropology and Aesthetics*, no. 42 (Autumn), pp. 159–165.

———. 2005 "Three Aztec Masks of the God Xipe," in *Thinking with Things: Toward a New Vision of Art*, pp. 209–224.

Pasztory, Esther, ed. 2002 *West by Nonwest*, in *RES: Anthropology and Aesthetics*, no. 42 (Autumn).

Walsh, J. M. 1997 "Crystal Skulls and Other Problems: Or, 'Don't Look It in the Eye'," in *Exhibiting Dilemmas: Issues of Representation at the Smithsonian*, eds. Amy Henderson and Adrienne L. Kaeppler. Washington & London: Smithsonian Institution Press, pp. 116–142.

———. 2008 "The Dumbarton Oaks Tlazolteotl: Looking Beneath the Surface," in *Journal de la Société des Américanistes.* Nanterre, France; pp. 7–43.

X. The Question of Indian Identity

Brandon, William. 1986 *New Worlds for Old: Reports from the New World and Their Effect on the Development of Social Thought in Europe, 1500–1800.* Athens, Ohio: Ohio University Press.

Johansen, Bruce E. 1982 *Forgotten Founders: How the American Indian Helped Shape Democracy.* Harvard, Mass.: Harvard Common Press.

Wetherford, Jack. 1958 *Indian Givers: How the Indians of the Americas Transformed the World.* New York: Crown Publishing Group.

XI. What One Needs to Know About Ancient American Art

Boone, Elizabeth H. 2000 *Stories in Red and Black: Pictorial Histories of the Aztecs and Mixtecs.* Austin: University of Texas Press.

———. 2007 *Cycles of Time and Meaning in the Mexican Books of Fate.* Joe R. and Teresa Lozano Long series in Latin American and Latino art and culture. Austin: University of Texas Press.

Coe, Michael D. 1962 *Mexico.* Ancient Peoples and Places Series, vol. 29. New York: Praeger.

———. 1966 *The Maya.* New York: Praeger.

D'Altroy, Terence. 2003 *The Incas.* Malden, MA: Blackwell Publishing.

Donnan, Christopher B. 2004 *Moche Portraits from Ancient Peru.* Austin: University of Texas Press.

Donnan, Christopher B., and Donna McClelland. 1999 *Moche Fineline Painting: Its Evolution and Aesthetics.* Los Angeles: UCLA Fowler Museum.

Gasparini, Graziano, and Luise Margolies. 1980 *Inca Architecture* trans. Patricia Lyon. Bloomington: Indiana University Press.

Miller, Mary Ellen. 1999 *Maya Art and Architecture.* New York: Thames & Hudson.

Moseley, Michael E. 2001 *The Incas and Their Ancestors: The Archaeology of Peru.* New York & London: Thames & Hudson.

Pasztory, Esther. 1983 *Aztec Art.* New York: H. N. Abrams.

———. 1997 *Teotihuacán: An Experiment in Living.* Norman: University of Oklahoma Press.

———. 1998 *Pre-Columbian Art.* New York: Cambridge University Press.

———. 2003 "Aztec Poetry," in *The Nahua Newsletter* 35 (February), pp. 20–23.

———. 2006 "A Civilization Going Mad—The Aztecs in Western Thought," in *Arqueología e historia del Centro de México—Homenaje a Eduardo Matos Moctezuma.* Leonardo López Luján, David Carrasco, Lourdes Cué, eds. Mexico City: Instituto Nacional de Antropología e Historia; pp. 637–644.

Stone-Miller, Rebecca. 1992 *To Weave for the Sun: Ancient Andean textiles in the Museum of Fine Arts, Boston.* New York & London: Thames & Hudson.

———. 1995 *Art of the Andes: From Chavín to Inca (World of Art Series).* New York: Thames & Hudson.

Urton, Gary. 2003 *Signs of the Inka Khipu: Binary Coding in the Andean Knotted-String Records.* Austin: University of Texas Press.

Winckelmann, Johann Joachim. 1764 *History of Ancient Art*, trans. G. Henry Lodge. Boston: James Munroe & Co. [1849].

Young-Sánchez, Margaret. 2004 *Tiwanaku: Ancestors of the Inca.* Denver: Denver Art Museum.

## XII. Epilogue

Haas, George J., and William R. Saunders. 2005 *The Cydonia Codex: Reflections from Mars.* Berkeley: Frog Ltd.

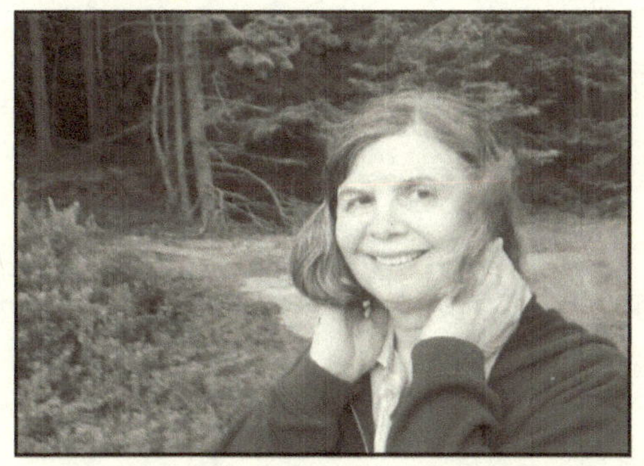
Photo by Richard Eaton

Esther Pasztory is Lisa and Bernard Selz Professor emeritus of pre-Columbian Art History and Archaeology at Columbia University. She has published extensively in the field of pre-Columbian art, including the first art historical manuscripts on Teotihuacan and the Aztecs. Born in Hungary, she emigrated to the United States in 1956, after the anti-Communist revolution. She attended Vassar College and Barnard Collage where she received a BA in art history. With her dissertation at Columbia, entitled *The Murals of Tepantitla, Teotihuacan*, she received her PhD in 1971. Esther now lives in Kennebunk, Maine.

www.ingramcontent.com/pod-product-compliance
Lightning Source LLC
LaVergne TN
LVHW051010080826
845145LV00009B/2555
*9781882190737*